I've coparented four  book had been avail releases parents from kids and gives permission to live a Jesus-oriented life in a family environment. With David's principles, parents and children can create a beautiful dance of journeying in faith together, learning from and with each other along the way.

> **Dr. Rowland Smith,** national director of Forge America, author, professor, and pastor

Studies are clear that the most impactful people in a child's life are their parents, and David Sunde has provided a fabulous resource to inspire us to take the next step in that journey. With clear insights but a kind tone, David shepherds parents through the holy ground of everyday discipleship with the kids God has given us.

> **Christie Thomas,** author of *Little Habits, Big Faith: How Simple Practices Help Your Family Grow in Jesus*

I've had the pleasure of spending hours with Dave Sunde to both talk and write about the ideas in this book. They are so helpful and relevant for families. He has provided an updated game plan for applying what God taught us through Moses in Deuteronomy and what Jesus modeled in the Gospels. I encourage you to take his challenge and practice these ideas for the sake of your family's health, your kids' growth, and God's Kingdom. As David says, disciplemaking begins at home.

> **Tim Elmore,** founder of Growing Leaders

David Sunde's *Homegrown Disciples* captures the heart of parenting as disciplemaking. By helping children follow Jesus, parents discover God's love and grace in deeper ways, growing in their own faith journeys. Sunde's seven rhythms offer practical, tangible tools for families to live out their faith together, weaving discipleship into daily life. With real-life examples and actionable practices, this book is a must-read for parents seeking to cultivate a home where faith flourishes—for their children and themselves.

    Dr. Teresa Roberts, DMin, professor of ministry and Christian formation and author of *Raising Disciples: Guiding Your Kids into a Faith of Their Own*

First, best book title ever! Second, I've worked with students and parents for over thirty years in the local church, and *this* is the book I've been waiting for! *Homegrown Disciples* makes the case and provides the tools and confidence for parents to be the primary spiritual influence in their children's lives. I'm grateful to David for providing such a wonderful resource for parents. I can't wait to share it with the parents at my church!

    Kurt Johnston, pastor of campus development at Saddleback Church

HOMEGROWN DISCIPLES

Parenting Rhythms for Drawing Your Kids into Life with God

David Sunde

Published in alliance with Tyndale House Publishers

NavPress.com

Homegrown Disciples: Parenting Rhythms for Drawing Your Kids into Life with God

Copyright © 2025 by David Sunde. All rights reserved.

A NavPress resource published in alliance with Tyndale House Publishers

NavPress is a registered trademark of NavPress, The Navigators, Colorado Springs, CO. The NavPress logo is a trademark of NavPress, The Navigators, Colorado Springs, CO. *Tyndale* is a registered trademark of Tyndale House Ministries. Absence of ® in connection with marks of NavPress or other parties does not indicate an absence of registration of those marks.

The Team:
David Zimmerman, Publisher; Deborah Sáenz, Editor; Elizabeth Schroll, Copyeditor; Lacie Phillips, Production Assistant; Lindsey Bergsma, Designer; Sarah Ocenasek, Proofreading Coordinator

Cover illustration of Grandad's wisdom copyright © by Hellen Cooke/Stocksy. All rights reserved.

Author photo copyright © 2024 by David Sunde. All rights reserved.

All Scripture quotations, unless otherwise indicated, are taken from the Holy Bible, *New International Version*,® *NIV*.® Copyright © 1973, 1978, 1984, 2011 by Biblica, Inc.® Used by permission. All rights reserved worldwide. Scripture quotations marked KJV are taken from the *Holy Bible*, King James Version. Scripture quotations marked NASB are taken from the (NASB®) New American Standard Bible,® copyright © 1960, 1971, 1977, 1995, 2020 by The Lockman Foundation. Used by permission. All rights reserved. www.lockman.org.

The author is represented by the literary agency of WordServe Literary, www.wordserveliterary.com.

Some of the anecdotal illustrations in this book are true to life and are included with the permission of the persons involved. All other illustrations are composites of real situations, and any resemblance to people living or dead is purely coincidental.

For information about special discounts for bulk purchases, please contact Tyndale House Publishers at csresponse@tyndale.com, or call 1-855-277-9400.

ISBN 978-1-64158-817-1

Printed in the United States of America

31	30	29	28	27	26	25
7	6	5	4	3	2	1

To Annika, Bjørn & Clara.
God has a middle name, and you reveal all the ways He is with us.
"There was nothing worth sharing
like the love that let us share our name!"
(The Avett Brothers, "Murder in the City")

Contents

INTRODUCTION **PARENTS AS DISCIPLEMAKERS** *1*

CHAPTER 1 **A RHYTHM OF APPRENTICING** *15*

CHAPTER 2 **A RHYTHM FOR RENEWAL** *39*

CHAPTER 3 **A RHYTHM OF HOSPITALITY** *63*

CHAPTER 4 **A RHYTHM IN COMMUNITY** *85*

CHAPTER 5 **A RHYTHM OF COMPASSION** *105*

CHAPTER 6 **A RHYTHM OF GENEROSITY** *127*

CHAPTER 7 **A RHYTHM OF GRATITUDE** *145*

CHAPTER 8 **CROWNED AND COMMISSIONED** *167*

NOTES *178*

INTRODUCTION

PARENTS AS DISCIPLEMAKERS

Seeding Eternity in the Everydayness of Our Life with Kids

CAN YOU IMAGINE a morning routine that feels like a sacred liturgy?

If you're in the thick of raising kids right now, this probably sounds ridiculous. Mornings are typically a blur of matching socks, making lunches, packing bags, and feeling relieved if the kids brush their teeth. You're just trying to get out the door on time without too many tears. But mornings are also a fleeting window of opportunity to set a tone for your family and commission your kids into the world.

Some of my most cherished memories of parenting are from beginning our days together: seated around our island counter with peanut butter toast, smoothies, or bowls of cereal as my wife, Laurel, and I would go over spelling words with my daughter or math problems with my son. Before the coffee kicked in, I'd often lean on a morning playlist to bring the energy—and maybe create an anthem—in anticipation of a new day. Songs often provide the words and images to ground us before we jump into what lies ahead. One tune by the Avett Brothers, curiously called "Murder in the City," became a recurring psalm for my family. It has a brilliant stop-what-we're-doing, everyone-join-in chorus that I'd always make our kids sing along with:

> *Always remember there was nothing worth sharing*
> *like the love that let us share our name.*[1]

The lyrics mirrored the message I tried to instill in my kids daily: Family is sacred, even if we didn't treat each other well the night before or that morning.

What if your home could become God's primary laboratory where all who enter get to experiment and experience His unconditional love? It's about having boundaries *and* mercy, mixing truth *with* grace, creating walls *and* maintaining gates. This may sound easier said than done, especially if you feel exhausted and overwhelmed in this season. But trust me when I say that this is not only possible but also a primary way God anchors our identity and nurtures our soul-deep need for belonging.

If you've been in a Christian context for a while, you likely already know that disciplemaking involves learning to share what you already have with the people around you. It's learning to talk about the difference Christ is making in you, animating the life of Christ. To animate is to incarnate. Just as God took on flesh and blood to live among us in sending His Son, we also can become the tangible presence of Christ in how we influence others. We tend to think about disciplemaking as helping other adult believers grow in their faith, which is one accurate definition of the term. But we can also apply the disciplemaking paradigm to the role of a parent or guardian. In fact, parenting is the quintessential relationship for spiritually reproducing a living faith.

And Immanuel, literally "God with us," offers the ultimate example of spiritual reproduction.[2] God is with us as we seek to mirror living faith with our kids. God guides us as we guide them. He reveals the depth of His love as a heavenly parent as we invest our love, whether our children notice, appreciate, or receive our affection in the moment. And He is with us in spiritually leading—ever so graciously—even (perhaps especially) when we do so imperfectly. Disciplemaking is not a zero-sum game where all the benefit goes to the one being invested in. Disciplemaking becomes a way God reveals more about His character, grace, and presence as we share our lives for the sake of others.

And He's with our children as they experience the Father's care through us. Reframing parenting as disciplemaking helps us be more intentional in how we help our children experience God's "touch"—His heart and presence, His truth and grace. This is not only for their well-being and eternal trajectory but for ours as well. The Resurrection doesn't just offer new life; it offers us do-overs! Chances to begin again, both as parent-disciplemakers and as children of God, and to help us experience the reach—even the unfairness—of grace.

God taps the verbally clumsy, the spiritually uncoordinated, and the domestic underachievers among us and graciously suggests that we still have what it takes to be like Him.

Our shortcomings don't change the name we bear.

Our faults don't disqualify us from disciplemaking.

We are adopted. Beloved.

And He calls us His own. God is parenting us while we parent our children.

Sometimes as parents we think we need to adopt a rigid Christian parenting philosophy or deliver enough of the "right" content to our children for them to embrace the faith. We may think we need to find a church with the most exciting children's theater or youth program to keep their attention. Or that we need to try to shelter them for as long as possible by limiting their exposure to culture's divergent messaging and values. None of these efforts or concerns are wrong, and all of them illustrate the weight we feel while making decisions that can impact our children and their faith. There are no easy answers, but there's also a different approach.

We raise homegrown disciples by cultivating God's revelation in daily and even ordinary ways. It's about learning to see the Kingdom's signs, illustrate God's heart, and animate His story.

It might be startling to think that Jesus never said, "Follow My teaching."

He simply said, "Follow Me."[3]

Jesus extended the relational invitation of presence. Similarly, the power of your unique parenting relationship and proximity is that you are offering your kids a relational invitation to grow in faith together, day by day.

If we reduce discipleship to a program, all we can measure are results. Did you get through the curriculum? How many showed up? Can you remember what you read, heard, or (hopefully) learned? But it's when we frame disciplemaking as a developmental relationship that we can measure fruit. Results are the things that happen around us, but fruit is what happens inside us. Content isn't the key to changing hearts. Knowledge is important, but the Bible often implies the meaning of knowledge as relational. And in relationships—like those with kids coming of age—are the most fertile hearts to make Christ known in daily and ordinary ways. Again, it's not because we always get it right but because we let our kids be part of our growing relationship with Christ while we guide them.

There is a universally understood, largely unspoken truth

bomb that every parent can relate to. It's something that's exploded in my face many times over, leaving me vacillating between elation, guilt, optimism, doubt, pride, and gratitude. Ready for it? Here goes . . .

> *Sometimes our kids make us feel like we're way better parents than we really are.*
>
> *Other times our kids make us feel like we're way worse parents than we really are.*
>
> *And somewhere in the middle is the truth!*

This book is about cultivating that fertile middle ground.

We can't ensure our kids' faith, but we can cultivate the soil of our hearts and homes. This is what raising homegrown disciples is all about! Rather than scrambling to raise happy kids or sacrificing to help them excel, we can make our home a studio for discovering God's heart.

Too many parenting resources assume we're desperate for advice and offer an emotional Heimlich as a cure. Often this so-called cure takes the form of a pathway to achieve optimal outcomes for our kids' lives.

Feeling inadequate or like we're not keeping up are never helpful motivators. Fear is just the shadow side of being unfamiliar. But we shouldn't confuse being new with being unqualified and unable. We disciple like we parent—with God's grace—learning as we go, one day at a time. I pray to see God use the role of parenting to reveal the Father's love for you and shape and guide your disciplemaking adventures. We develop awareness of God's presence similarly to how we nurture our own presence in our children's lives: by looking for opportunities to spend time together throughout the day. Parenting is a lot of things, but the most significant reality is this: *God uses our children to teach us about His sacrificial love.*

Our heavenly Father wants us to impart a living faith to our kids . . . and to reveal aspects of His heart for us through our children. There's nothing like raising kids to remind us that we aren't intended to be at the center of our lives. Equally, our kids should be a priority but not the center of our lives. If we spent twenty-four hours each day advocating for our kids' well-being, we still couldn't secure it. We can't control the outcome of our disciplemaking efforts. But we aren't in this alone: God wants to teach us through children's eyes.

He is parenting us the same way we are parenting them.

A MIRROR WORKS EVEN WITH OUR EYES CLOSED

We are already reproducing ourselves to our kids, whether we mean to or not. Our kids observe our trust, hope, commitment, and priorities firsthand. They also see us display skepticism, negativity, a temper, or a scarcity mindset, and sometimes they reflect these attitudes back to us. When it comes to family, there's no place to hide. We mirror our faith, politics, grudges, biases, and cultural preferences. We can't hide our enthusiasm and priorities (or lack thereof). They don't even need to be stated. Kids learn what we value by how we act and react, what we say and don't say.

Many parents feel uneasy when it comes to being a spiritual leader. (If that's you, kudos to you for reading this far!) Being a spiritual leader probably feels more daunting than teaching manners, modeling a healthy lifestyle, or helping your kids excel in school or with a sport or performing art. Parents are natural advocates in most areas of our kids' lives. With gnawing FOMO temptations, we badly want to help them get ahead! However, parents too often feel like they run out of runway before effectively taking off with their children's faith development.

May I suggest that you're probably further along than you think?

And you're not alone. This is both the beauty and the vulnerability of our lives together. This resource is intended to be a field guide for parents in the trenches desiring to point their kids in the right direction.

WORKING WITH WHAT YOU HAVE

This is not a disclaimer, but it should be disarming for any pressures, obligations, and inadequacies you might feel as a parent: *Parenting as disciplemaking is simply working with what you have.*

The greatest leverage every parent has is influence and proximity. I'm confident that "he who began a good work in you will carry it on to completion" (Philippians 1:6). We don't need to hold family meetings to teach important spiritual lessons. Jesus didn't preach forty-five-minute, three-point sermons. He simply lived His life in proximity to others. Each day, Jesus found ways to illustrate what the Kingdom of God looks like using everyday metaphors, stories, and images. Where did Jesus get that way of discipling from? Jesus discipled within a rich oral storytelling culture where the Scriptures were more heard and memorized communally than read and studied individually. Additionally, an apprenticing framework was embedded in Hebraic culture. When we think of disciplemaking in Jesus' time, we might envision someone sitting at the feet of a rabbi, learning from what they had to say. But Jesus reveals disciplemaking to be much more: Disciplemakers invite others into the shadow of their daily lives, teaching not only with their words but also with their actions. Disciplemakers intentionally invite others to participate in their daily activities. They do life together—much like parents do life with their kids, day by day. The Hebrew Scriptures therefore offer a natural way for parents and guardians to plant seeds, spark imagination, and illustrate God's care and presence.

This field guide is a resource to inspire you and provide some imagination for discipling your children into life with Christ. I hope it's more incarnational than instructional. Rather than expecting you to simply parrot my lessons, I trust that God's been writing a story in you. So what if we think about disciplemaking this way . . . ?

You are the syllabus.
And your life experience in Christ is the curriculum.
Disciplemakers teach what they know and reproduce who they are.

Being a disciplemaker doesn't mean you've arrived at your faith destination; rather, it means finding ways to impart what you have already picked up along your journey toward Christlikeness. This approach to disciplemaking is the most authentic form of spiritual reproduction, a truth that can't be disputed.

> *You are the syllabus.*
> *And your life experience in Christ is the curriculum.*
> *Disciplemakers teach what they know and reproduce who they are.*

Finding our footing for spiritual leadership begins by being attentive to seeing the Kingdom of God around us. Over time, our hearts get resensitized to the Spirit's prompts. Interruptions become divine appointments. Challenges emerge as teachable moments. Wins feel more like grace than entitlement. We cultivate a growing awareness of God's presence only to discover, once again, He's with us in the hard and the good.

FOUR WINDOWS FOR EVERYDAY DISCIPLEMAKING

Most Christians are familiar with the command to "love the LORD your God with all your heart and with all your soul and with all your strength" (Deuteronomy 6:5). It comes from a sacred daily prayer called the Shema that God's people would pray in Moses' time.[4] The sixty-four-thousand-dollar question is *How on earth do you do that?* Read more of the prayer, and we can figure out how:

> *These commandments that I give you today are to be on your hearts. Impress them on your children. Talk about them* **when you sit** *at home and* **when you walk** *along the road,* **when you lie down** *and* **when you get up.***
>
> DEUTERONOMY 6:6-7, *emphasis added*

The Shema outlines natural teachable moments—or windows of time—woven into each day: **dinnertime, travel time, bedtime,** and **morning time.**[5] Let's look at each window in turn.

"When you sit": Think of dinnertime as a cherished standing appointment. It's an ideal way to stay current with your family by asking questions, telling on yourself, laughing together, and listening to what's being said—and *not* being said—by your kids.

"When you walk": Approach your travel time as a faith journey. If you ever feel like a taxi driver shuttling your kids to and from school and extracurricular activities, know that all that time on the road isn't wasted. You can redeem it by singing praise songs, debriefing each other's days, asking open-ended questions, and praying together at drop-offs. If you're facing a deadline or a hard conversation at work, ask your kids to pray for you!

"When you lie down": Consider bedtime a sacred ritual. If your child is young, after they brush their teeth and settle in, listen to a song that declares God's worth (let your child select one from a handful of suggestions). Read a storybook that reinforces God's love, and then pray together. For prayer times, we liked to have our kids say a random number of things they were grateful for. With older kids, you may want to pray for friends looking for work, struggling in their marriages, battling sickness, or grieving losses. Bedtime is typically the most tender time for conversations. As your kids grow into adolescence, they may be more comfortable asking hard questions during this window.

"When you get up": Imagine morning time as a daily commission. Set the tone for the day with a playlist to wake up your kids and remind them of what's true. Speak to their potential. Instead of just telling them you love them, tell them some specific things you love about them. ("I see how much you love reading, storytelling, art, and building things. God showed creativity in creating the world, and I can see that He made you to be creative too. That reflects His image." "I see you as such a caring and loyal friend that it reminds me how God is always with us, no matter what." "Hearing you laugh and seeing you smile is God's way of bringing me joy." "When you're patient or share with your sister, you make our family better.") How is God revealing Himself to you through them? Send them off with His love with your words!

Again, God is parenting us as we parent our children.

As we continue exploring this topic, we will use the Shema to help us work out practical applications in our parenting rhythms. At the end of each chapter, I offer ways to engage with your children at dinnertime, travel time, bedtime, and morning time. These are disciplemaking windows where you have the opportunity to give words to faith, till the soil of your kids' hearts, and embody the Good News.

I also provide an interactive section called "Finding Your Rhythm" so that you, as a parent, can create a longer runway to take off and land faith conversations with your kids.

FINDING A FAMILY RHYTHM FOR "GOD WITH US"

In the coming pages, I want to fan the flame for you to reimagine parenting as disciplemaking. As you'll find, Scripture reveals teachable moments in what we're already doing in our everyday family lives. The idea of being a spiritual leader can be daunting. Similarly, playing the role of disciplemaker can feel foreign. For many, the concept of discipleship is acquired through sermons and books. For others, it's about church attendance, connecting in a small group, and volunteering in church ministry. All those things are helpful. But the most critical aspect of discipleship is spiritual reproduction. Jesus didn't set out to win the masses or reach the world. He had a focused relational strategy to train the few to reach the many. Most of Jesus' recorded ministry was not in a classroom or even indoors. It was outside and part of daily life. Proximity to their rabbi shaped His disciples. He didn't call them to follow a creed or doctrine. He invited them to follow Him!

Jesus is the Living Word. What we discover about growth and change is this:

We don't *think* our way into a new way of living.

We *live* our way into a new way of thinking.

Here's another way to think about it: What is belief without action? (James 2:14). As parents, we might ask ourselves, *Am I living in a way that encourages my children toward faith, compassion, and reliance on Jesus?*

In this book, I offer seven rhythms to help disciplemaking parents live out their faith:

- **apprenticing** (following Jesus while inviting others);
- **renewal** (learning to recognize God's voice);
- **hospitality** (making room for new faces in new places);
- **community** (making each other better by saving our best for family);
- **compassion** (learning to give because we all have needs);
- **generosity** (sharing with others what already belongs to God); and
- **gratitude** (showing our thanks in big and small ways).

My hope is that these rhythms will help you find fresh, kid-friendly language for your faith practices. I also offer practical expressions to guide you as in the spiritual leadership of your home. These rhythms help us not only to know *about* God but also, hopefully, to experience Him. They help us imagine ways to leverage faith for the benefit of others, particularly our children. These disciplemaking rhythms offer a way to reproduce a *living* faith in our kids' lives, not just a Sunday-go-to-church faith.

My goal in this field guide is not to be theologically exhaustive but rather to be deeply practical. We are attempting to discover the sacred already present in our ordinary lives. Childhood is precious. Each stage has new challenges to tackle and joys to cherish. In the thick of parenting, it can be easy to get so caught up in the current stages our kids are in that we go into survival mode, just doing the next thing needed to keep them healthy and happy. And it's okay to want those outcomes for our kids. But we mustn't forget our long-term goal: kids who know and love Christ and who make Him known to others. In the end, Christian parenting is about seeing ourselves as sending agents. Here's to finding Christ in your homegrown disciplemaking journey!

We don't think our way into a new way of living. We live our way into a new way of thinking.

CHAPTER 1

A RHYTHM OF APPRENTICING

Following Jesus While Inviting Followers

PARENTING IS ARGUABLY a person's most sacred investment, greatest sacrifice, and most significant legacy. When our daughter, Annika, was born nearly two years after our son, I began a journal for her as an attempt to nurture our daddy-daughter relationship. I was also restless about raising pastor's kids, who often unfairly spend too many hours at church and draw the gaze of parishioners. I wanted to instill in them a living faith, a love for Jesus, not simply a Sunday-go-to-church faith. I had a distinct impression, which I took as a prompt from the Lord: *You've got it half right.*

I felt the Spirit saying, *Yes, be Christ to her. But I also want to teach you about Me through her, so take note!* God would disciple me as I discipled my kids.

So, for thirteen years, I kept a handwritten chronicle of God's

Spirit reflecting to me like an animated mirror. It became a valuable practice of God resensitizing my heart. Many of the stories I share in this book are from those encounters. Here's one from my Annika journal:

> "We had a tough morning." Those were your words as you climbed in the car, headed for school drop-off. You were right, but it wasn't *we* as much as *me*. This was *not* my finest hour. In my effort to make breakfast, pack lunches, help finish homework, shower, and get everyone ready for the day . . . it was regrettable. Your words were gentle but spot-on . . . and convicting! You weren't condemning but empathizing. After dropping you and Bjørn off and having a moment of reflection, I thought of your words. Spoken most graciously and gently, they were a timely reminder that God sees. He's near, and we still have each other to experience God's love. Thanks for being Christ to me amid it all.
>
> *XOXO,*
> *Daddy*
>
> LETTER TO NINE-YEAR-OLD ANNIKA
> APRIL 15, 2010

Christians are called to make disciples. I've noticed that most churches believe they are answering God's call to make disciples. Yet many earnest Christians—those who have experienced the whole range of church teaching, community life, service, giving, and worship—lack the confidence to disciple new or younger believers. As I've leaned into this alarming observation, I often hear from those same people that they have never been discipled. Maybe this is because programs don't disciple people; people disciple people. So unless a Christ follower has another Christian take them under their wing, they will struggle to animate the life of Christ—mind, body, and Spirit—in their life.

Simply put, every disciple is a believer, but not every believer is a disciple.

A person can believe in God, mentally assenting to Christ's lordship, without reorienting any desire, attitude, motivation, or behavior. One can believe and remain selfish, untrusting, controlling, and mean. Christians originally were known as people of "the Way" (Acts 24:14). The Enlightenment introduced the idea of a rational religion of believers. But belief is more than just acknowledging God's existence in our minds. After all, "even the demons believe [that there is one God]—and shudder" (James 2:19).

Please hear me: I'm a great enthusiast of the local church. So much good comes from local expressions of the body of Christ. But if the boldest expression of faith is a Sunday event, it will never adequately equip the saints for everyday life beyond church walls.

Many churches have exciting youth programs, but these are not meant to serve as the primary faith education children receive. When parents rely on church programs to disciple their kids, they train their kids to be confident only in inviting someone to church. This kind of faith will only take them so far.

No one is better situated to disciple a child than the people responsible for caring for that child every day. Just as God is with us (remember Immanuel?), we are invited to not just be witnesses of His love—we're called to "with-ness."[1] Children are "with-nesses" so that we can be who God has called us to be! The daily proximity, relational influence, and incarnational presence can reveal the Kingdom of God on earth without equal.

I'm glad you're willing to join me on this journey as we reframe parenting as homegrown disciplemaking, where we partner with God to draw our kids into life with Him. The following pages offer ways for parents to have eyes to see and prepare to reproduce our experiences with God. It might seem odd, at first, to reconsider how you view parenting, but let this truth sink in:

God is discipling us as we disciple our kids.

REFRAMING PARENTING

I like to think of discipling our kids as apprenticing within a trade. *Apprenticeship* is tradespeople's language for a working relationship where a less experienced (often younger) person learns a skill by shadowing another person experienced in that area as they go about their workweek. It implies an on-the-job, hands-on approach and real-time training in the skill set.

Apprenticing is not about encouraging others to look, talk, act, and even believe identically to us. Instead, apprenticeship in a parenting context simply means letting our kids observe where our hope abides. It's manifesting the presence of Jesus—not from a position of power and knowledge but by humbly and faithfully following God's guidance—with tender intentionality. The beauty of homegrown discipleship lies in our proximity to our kids and relational capital formed by the time, energy, and love we share. It's all about setting the forms for faith and discipleship before the wet cement hardens.

Apprenticing works shoulder to shoulder more than face to face.

Apprenticing works shoulder to shoulder more than face to face.

In this book I use the words *apprenticing* and *disciplemaking* interchangeably. While there might be some nuance, both terms are active and dynamic, implying progression from one state to another. In the ancient world, a disciple was more than just a student of a rabbi's faith life; they were to learn about the rabbi's whole life. Rabbis served as spiritual parents of their students.

In the Gospels we see Jesus engaging in this kind of apprenticing relationship with the Twelve. By including them in His daily conversations, requests, and interruptions, Jesus taught the disciples what it means to embody a living faith. And in turn, the disciples did the same for others, ultimately spreading—through apprenticeship—what became known as Christianity throughout the known world.

In the story of Jesus feeding the five thousand, many people assume the story's focus is on the large crowd of people who are fed. But remember, most of these people were probably unaware that a miracle was occurring. If you think about it, this miracle actually seems pretty unremarkable because the demonstration was mostly hidden. The masses were gathered in a field without a public address system. They had no cameras or stadium monitors. Whom do you think this miracle was for if most people were likely unaware that fish and loaves were multiplied? The crowd didn't know how many fish Jesus started with; those folks were just happy to get a free meal. But the Twelve acted as ushers in a sea of people. They were likely the only ones who realized the baskets weren't running out of fish and chips! This story is an example of how Jesus masterfully created environments to train His disciples behind the scenes while also meeting the needs of those coming to Him for help. Jesus was imparting in His disciples a living faith that would lead to spiritual multiplication down the road.

JESUS' IDEA

One of my former pastors introduced me to a framework for apprenticing based on Jesus' example of training the few to train many. Jesus' strategy didn't involve a classroom but an IDEA.[2] He offered the disciples instruction (*I*), demonstrated (*D*) what He intended them to learn, and gave them experience (*E*) as part of their trial and error. Then, like a thoughtful parent, He took them aside afterward to debrief and offer an assessment (*A*). As Christian parents, our role is to disciple the few (our children) in a way that will lead them to someday impart their faith to others.

Let's look at each of the four ingredients of Jesus' IDEA and see how this framework can help us raise our kids to experience the reality of Christ through us.

I: *Instruction*

Instruction is typically given in a theoretical context to prepare someone for what might (or will) happen in the future. It's interesting to observe how few of the Gospel stories occur indoors. Most of the recorded life of Christ and His disciplemaking happens in real-time encounters along the way to another location. The classroom is not divorced from the laboratory. This is the salient point for parents: Rather than teaching our children what to do or not do, we must teach them the *who*, *why*, and *what* of Jesus in everyday life.

Jesus made a way for us to be forgiven, experience the grace of second chances, and take His name and likeness within God's family. As we give our lives to the rule and reign of Christ, it changes the desires of our hearts toward the longings of the Father. He gives us a new way to be human in restoring a world fractured by sin, greed, power, deceit, and death. He came to inaugurate the Kingdom of Heaven on earth, where Christians are invited to live as ambassadors as we await the return of the King to restore all things.

Instruction from parents is also about explaining the difference Jesus is making in your life. It explains why you do what you do and how Jesus has helped you reshape your desires, form new convictions, and establish new priorities. Teaching your kids the *why* of Jesus is as critical as explaining the *what* of Jesus. In addition to instilling what you believe, try to answer how you came to believe it. This can make faith more personal—and therefore more magnetic.

D: *Demonstration*

If instruction explains the *who*, *what*, and *why* of Jesus, then demonstration is the *how*. After all, what is belief without action? James asks, "What good is it if someone claims to have faith but has no deeds as evidence?" (James 2:14, author's paraphrase). Before the disciples left the nest, they were invited to shadow Jesus. They were ushers at the feeding of the five thousand, sideline observers of healings and deliverances. And they were allowed to be like flies on the wall as Jesus had difficult conversations. Similarly, our kids' best way of learning is when they shadow us and begin to understand how we live out our faith. They need to see what compassion, forgiveness, generosity, and hospitality look like as expressions of a living faith in God. As it was with Jesus, demonstration is where the Word becomes flesh in us (John 1:14).

E: *Experience*

By demonstrating what a life on mission looks like in everyday ways, Jesus gave His disciples valuable experience while they were together. He gave them power and authority to do the work (Luke 9:1), the same resources Christians have today. Jesus gave the Twelve increasingly more agency to participate in caring for others. The experience of serving others is part of how we might know what God's love is like.

Many of us live in neighborhoods and attend school and church with people who have similar economic and educational profiles. Laurel and I wanted our kids to experience crossing typical social divides. From when they were toddlers until the present, we have planned times to connect with unhoused populations, greeting them in the early morning with coffee, socks, and ramen. We hosted regular Supper Clubs to share meals with residents of subsidized housing. And as the immigration crisis developed, we found creative ways to express hospitality to recent immigrants, many of whom remain dear friends to this day.

A: *Assessment*

After the feeding-of-the-masses miracle, Jesus gathered with the disciples to debrief their encounter. This is one of many times we see Jesus assessing an experience with the Twelve. As our own experience with Christ deepens, it helps to think out loud with kids about the lessons we're learning. The more we tell on ourselves, the more likely it is that our kids will be willing to receive feedback and even correction from us. Debriefing our own choices, reactions, and attitudes is not about staking our reputation as parents. Instead, it's about helping our children understand that God is always present and is looking to reflect His love, care, and compassion through each one of us.

BEING ATTENTIVE TO THE ORDINARY

Having your children apprentice you in the faith can seem intimidating to many parents. But I invite you to remember that much of the apprenticeship process is quite ordinary. It will require us, however, to be attentive.

Moses knew a thing or two about attentiveness. Before Moses became a leader of the Jewish people, he was a shepherd. Keeping the flock safe required vigilance: watching for predators and other threats to the sheep in Moses' care. One day, while tending his flock, he came upon a bush that was actively burning yet was not being consumed. As Moses stared at this awesome sight, God spoke to him for the first time. A common interpretation of this biblical narrative is that God used the burning bush to attract Moses' attention. But suppose you were God and could do anything you wanted—split the Red Sea, make the sun stand still, set up a pillar of fire. Compared to such grand displays, the marvel of keeping a burning bush from being destroyed is less extraordinary. So why did God choose such a modest miracle?

Maybe the burning bush wasn't a miracle but a test.

God wanted to find out if Moses could see the divine in something as ordinary as a bush on fire. To see it as a miracle, Moses had to watch the flames long enough to realize that the branches were not being consumed. Moses didn't hear God speak until *after* he'd stopped to watch the burning bush for a while. In Moses' season in the desert, God was preparing him for spiritual leadership of a nation.

Similarly, God invites parents to discover the divine in ordinary encounters with our kids. Parenting is like feeling our way through the darkness, searching for the light switch. We learn how to parent by parenting. God wasn't providing light or warmth for Moses with the burning bush but direction. Victorian poet Elizabeth Barrett Browning writes, "Earth's crammed with heaven, / And every common bush afire with God; / But only he who sees, takes off his shoes."[3]

When Moses was told to remove his sandals in Exodus 3:5, the Hebrew word translated as "take off" or "remove" (*nashal*) can also be translated as "drop off" or "clear away." Like a person noticing they just tracked mud onto the living room carpet while guests are arriving, I think Moses discovered in that moment that he'd been standing on holy ground all along.

Holy ground can feel exactly like any other ground. This is

why the apprenticing approach to parenting is the most natural in the most ordinary setting of everyday life. Sometimes standing on holy ground feels like standing in a pile of manure of regrettable reactions and desired do-overs. But manure also makes a good fertilizer for new growth. It reminds us that nothing is for nothing.

> Disciplemaking is more organic and opportunistic than teaching outlines and curriculum.
> It isn't about teaching all the right lessons but talking about the lessons you've learned.
> It's telling on yourself without talking about what you've achieved or gotten away with.
> It's about capturing metaphors that stick more than Bible memorization.
> It's incarnating Christ by demonstrating that He is personable, familiar, tangible, and approachable.

As far as I can tell, Scripture doesn't speak to the "arrival" concept; faith is a lifelong journey. God is writing a story in us as His children and through us as we raise our children. There's no spiritual retirement in the Kingdom of God. We can celebrate how far we've come but also live with the reality of our shortcomings. This makes parenting a formative laboratory for us to experiment with God's grace as both apprentices and disciplemakers. That's good news!

LETTING GO AND TRUSTING THE PROCESS

Having our children apprentice us may seem counterintuitive in a Western, industrialized, and educated society where schools mass-produce learning. Apprenticing is more about shadowing. Our kids learn so much more than what we think we teach them. They learn because they have unfettered access to our lives. And this is what makes disciplemaking parenting so compelling. Life doesn't allow us to plan every discipleship lesson for our kids. But God prepares us as we prepare them.

When you send a child off to college, you live with a tension of excitement for them and a loss of control for you. If you have control tendencies or are a planner by nature, know this: When our daughter left for college, the only things we could plan for were her first tuition payment and her move-in date. Honestly, it was worse than the first day of kindergarten. You're left wondering, *Is my child ready? Am I?* Then you can't wait to hear from them. When Annika called once early during freshman year, my fears were allayed by her humble brag. Since phone calling wasn't her digital-native dialect of texting, I knew that what she had to say was newsworthy.

"Dad, I think I learned more about being handy and fixing stuff from you than we thought," Annika shared.

"What happened?" I asked.

"Well, I made some new friends, and we planned to find a church to attend together. There were five of us, and I was the first pickup. But the girl driving called me to say her car wouldn't start. So I ran across campus. I tried to start it, but there wasn't even a sound. So I told my friend, 'Your battery is dead.' My friend asked, 'How do you know that?' I said, 'Well, it doesn't make any sound at all. It's no big deal. Do you have jumper cables?' My friend said, 'Umm, no.'"

"So what'd you do?" I asked her.

"I explained, 'All we need to do is wave down some guy in a pickup truck and ask if we can use his jumper cables.' My friend said, 'Uh, I don't think that's a thing.' To which I said, 'It's totally a thing!'"

With that, Annika went on to describe how she scanned the nearest intersection and, with her five-foot-two-inch petite frame, smiled big and waved her arms like she was back in the dance line at halftime. She flagged down a full-size crew cab truck with a scrawny eighteen-year-old boy behind the wheel. She continued: "So I said, 'Hey, my friend's car battery died. Do you have any jumper cables?' The guy replied, 'Sorry . . . I don't think I do.' I said, 'Uh, I'm pretty sure you do. Do you mind if I look?' I didn't even wait for a reply. I opened the back door and folded the seat forward. And there they were!"

I beamed with pride as I listened to Annika tell this story. She continued: "The guy sheepishly said, 'Oh, cool . . . lemme help . . .' But I told him not to worry, that I had it. I could tell he was a little embarrassed he hadn't helped, so I let him roll up the cables and close the hood. Sure enough, the car started! My friend looked at me and asked, 'Who are you???' The best part, Dad, is that we weren't even late for church!"

And all along I thought she was distracted by watching dog, baby, and makeup videos on her phone. The lessons our kids pick up can feel as random as a spontaneous potluck menu. It makes me wonder whether our heavenly Father feels the same way about us as parent-disciples. God's revelation is all around us, yet there's no way to predict how seeds of truth in the soil of grace will deepen a system of roots. All we can do is keep seeding our kids' hearts with eternity and trusting the Spirit to bring forth fruit on earth.

PREPARING > PLANNING

I had no plan for my daughter to become handy or mechanically minded. I'm more of a carpenter than a mechanic, but my wife and I did involve Annika in DIY projects and household maintenance.

A RHYTHM OF APPRENTICING

Laurel and I had no plan to encourage a natural introvert to step up with boldness. Laurel has a music degree, so we planned for Annika to be musical. But on her own, she discovered a love of American Sign Language and worked at a deaf-owned restaurant.

Life doesn't always go as planned, but that doesn't mean we can't be prepared. We can adapt to our reality by reacting to changing situations, redeeming moments, and revealing how God's at work. One thing Laurel and I try to do in our lives—and this is our constant prayer—is grow awareness of God's presence. We don't know what tomorrow will bring, which makes it hard to battle perfectionism or control tendencies. But knowing that God is already present and at work? We want to keep learning to discern the signs.

There's a particular verse that many Christians like to cling to when they feel out of control or the future seems uncertain: "'I know the plans I have for you,' declares the Lord, 'plans to prosper you and not to harm you, plans to give you hope and a future'" (Jeremiah 29:11). For people who don't like surprises, there's comfort in hearing there's a plan. But what's supposed to happen in the meantime, when we experience more chaos than control?

The Hebrew word translated "plans" in Jeremiah 29:11 (*machashabah*) can connote a weaving image. Picture a tapestry with two very distinct sides. On one side are chaotic threads crisscrossing, making little sense. This side is hidden against a wall. On the other side, those same threads weave together a beautiful image made to be on display. The image we can see is the pretty side. It's discernible, pleasant, and tells a story. The back side, on the other hand, feels like the tension we live with. It's easy to see how this metaphor might play out in our personal and family lives. When our interior lives feel chaotic and messy, we may doubt that something good lies on the other side of the mess. But God's plans are good regardless of which side of the tapestry we're on.

He's always at work in our lives. Sometimes we see the good but miss the struggle. Other times, we're in the midst of the struggle and fail to see the good in it. Behind our front doors, our homes may be like the back side of a tapestry. What an unexpected visitor encounters may not be pretty, but that doesn't mean it isn't good.

Being spiritually prepared is about weaving together what you know about who God is to help your kids (and yourself!) discover how He is present.

The more we respond, yield, and/or turn to the prompts of God's Spirit, the more our lives are shaped. Homegrown disciple-making is less about controlling preferred outcomes than about responding to what's happening in the moment, realizing how God is already present! These are the lessons we can't plan for, but—in the moment—we can notice what God is doing in hopes of pointing our kids to Him.

PERSPECTIVE FUELS POTENTIAL

Discipling kids is like throwing a pass in football. We don't want to throw to where they are but to give them a lead for where they will be. It's normal for parents to encourage their kids' gifts and strengths and to provide opportunities to help them succeed. An apprenticing parenting approach adds another dimension to help our kids see what they can't see or understand on their own. It is about instilling acceptance and value beyond their performance. An apprenticing relationship allows us to be part of a learning curve that teaches us as we guide our kids.

Our family normalized what we called "two-degree talks" to speak to who our kids could become in Christ. Sometimes—on a family date night, while over dinner, or tucking them into bed—my wife and I shared "I see . . ." statements about the good our kids were capable of. More than simply praising performance, Laurel and I tried to ground our kids in God's truth to help them weather storms of circumstances and how they might feel in a given moment. Here are a few examples you can use, adapt, and expand on to help you find your leadership voice at home:

- "I see in you a joy that is often a source of strength for me."
- "I see a level of trust in you that reminds me of what's possible."
- "I see you becoming a great dad (or mom) because of how you care for and enjoy little kids."
- "I see your character—you have a special ability to choose between right and wrong."
- "I see you becoming a leader to your peers, not as a loud voice but because of your character."
- "I see in you a strength—an unusual ability to stand alone because you believe it's the right thing."
- "I see in you compassion—you have a sensitive eye for people who are hurt or overlooked."
- "I see in you joy—a special ability to laugh out loud and lift people around you up."
- "I see in you security—you're comfortable in your own skin."

When a child (or any person, for that matter) hears someone they love speak to their potential, it motivates them to live into that truth. We want to put our kids on our shoulders by picturing things to come. Mostly, we want them to be able to align their story with God's ongoing hope. When we incorporate "I see . . ."

statements into our family rhythms, our children will learn how to do this for themselves—and hopefully someday it will be natural for them to speak into someone else's life in the same way you speak into theirs.

LEGACY BUILDING

I wonder if one reason the story of the Bible rings true is because it's about one human failure after another. That should encourage every parent who feels inadequate to lead spiritually and reproduce their faith. If we're going to receive and act on God's grace—if we're ever going to take a mulligan (a do-over) or rebuild our relationships—we need to reframe our approach to our own shortcomings. One thing that's true in marriage and family life is that we can't fake it. There's no pretense or hiding our insecurities, struggles, bad moods, or rough days.

When I lead engaged couples through premarital counseling, I always pose the same two questions. The first one is *How was conflict handled in your home growing up?* Responses have varied from "My parents gave each other the silent treatment" and "We didn't talk about things that bothered us" to "Shouting matches, door slamming, and name-calling were common." My point is this: *Conflict is the most natural thing in the world.* My follow-up question, *How did you see conflict resolved?*, often sparks puzzled looks, shoulder shrugs, or blank stares.

Everyone acquires a model for conflict resolution from their parents or guardians, but few of us grow up regularly witnessing healthy conflict resolution in action. When adults don't know how to regulate their own emotions or respond to others' emotions amid tough conversations, they don't feel equipped to teach the children in their care to do so. And some parents with good conflict resolution skills keep their arguments to themselves, afraid that hearing adults disagree might negatively impact children. But when our kids don't see us deal with hard things, we aren't adequately preparing them for life in the real world. And in the absence of our example, they may learn conflict resolution from TV or their peers, which doesn't help them develop this needed skill. Now, I'm not suggesting that we should resolve *all* conflicts in front of our kids. Some content isn't appropriate for young ears, and we must use discretion in the timing and location of certain conversations. But it's good for our kids to observe us resolving conflict healthily because Christ has given us this ministry of reconciliation (2 Corinthians 5:18). Psychologist Adam Grant explains,

> Although productive disagreement is a critical life skill, it's one that many of us never fully develop. The problem starts early: parents disagree behind closed doors, fearing that conflict will make children anxious or somehow damage their character. Yet research shows that how often parents argue has no bearing on their children's academic, social, or emotional development. What matters is how respectfully parents argue, not how frequently. Kids whose parents clash constructively feel more emotionally safe in elementary school, and over the next few years they actually demonstrate more helpfulness and compassion toward their classmates.[4]

However counterintuitive it may seem, you're actually doing the children in your care a favor when you don't hide that you're upset . . . especially when you thoughtfully address the issue at hand with the people involved, remembering that they, too, have been made in the image of God.

Scripture supports modeling healthy conflict resolution. We

find forgiveness touted in the Old Testament and the New. Jesus ranks the commandment to "love your neighbor as yourself" (Leviticus 19:18) as the second greatest, only subordinate to loving God. And reconciliation is at the heart of His story and mission. In His oft-quoted Sermon on the Mount, Jesus encourages us to ask God to "forgive us our debts, as we also have forgiven our debtors" (Matthew 6:12). The greatest deposit we parents can make in our kids is that of expanding their capacity to apologize and to offer forgiveness. That's why each time I offer premarital counseling, I tell the engaged couple, "The greatest legacy you can instill in your children is knowledge of how to give and receive forgiveness. Start practicing now, *before* they arrive."

An inheritance is something we leave for someone.
A legacy is what we leave in them.

The Resurrection is the hinge pin on which the doors of Christianity swing. It promises that we can begin again. Christianity animates new life by teaching Christ followers to overcome our debts, forgive as we've been forgiven. We can be defeated but not disqualified. Spiritual leadership is not about avoiding failure but about finding people to help you get back up when you fail.

The words *inheritance* and *legacy* are often used interchangeably. Both suggest that something of value is left behind after a person's life on earth is over. But there's one notable distinction.

An inheritance is something we leave *for* someone.

A legacy is what we leave *in* them.[5]

An apprenticing approach to parenting is about leaving a legacy. There are things that our children will inherit from my wife and me. Some are items of worth. Others are sentimental. All will have some value, at least to our kids, because of the life we share. The rhythm of apprenticing instills a legacy of what heaven on earth can look like in the children in our care. While we'll always feel like spiritual works in progress (because that's what we are!), the great question is *What can we do with what we have already experienced, learned, and overcome in our spiritual lives?*

FINDING YOUR RHYTHM: DISTILLING THE CHARACTER AND MISSION OF JESUS

As we develop a rhythm of having our children apprentice us, we should be able to distill the character and mission of Jesus into four things that any kid can grasp. Here is an impactful exercise in actively reading Scripture for themes and for signs about who Jesus is.

Start with the Gospel according to John. You can select a few chapters for the dinner table or for bedtime reading. Set aside ten minutes a day to uncover the layers of John's Gospel.

1. **Read each chapter for four themes.** John takes a different approach from the other Gospel writers in his testimony about Jesus: For the most part, John is more thematic in his arrangement of the narrative. He wants us to know that Jesus is, in fact, the Son of God. So he uses four descriptors: Jesus as the *Light*, *Life*, *Love*, and *Truth*. But it doesn't end there. Jesus' invitation to us for a better way of life is that, like Christ, we can also reflect that Light, which brings Life, that might resound with Love and share His Truth.

   As you read a chapter aloud, have your kids listen and interrupt you when they hear these four descriptive words. Try using four colored pencils (one color for each theme) and look for verses that contain each of those words.

Actively reading Scripture this way helps us see this familiar text closer to the way I think John intended. Any parent can communicate these four simple themes about who Christ is. And these four themes are simple enough that a child can understand them.

2. **Number each of Jesus' miracles.** John also writes in layers, or signs. As you identify the four themes of *Light*, *Life*, *Love*, and *Truth*, also label the seven miracles He performed during His earthly ministry. They reveal the power and authority of Christ progressively and—it could be argued—parallel to the Creation story in Genesis.

   Jesus' first miracle was turning water into wine at a wedding feast. If you were a first-century Israelite, you understood that the Mosaic covenant (think: the Ten Commandments) was a marriage of sorts between God and His people. John wants to share that there's a new covenant in Christ. Of course, the eighth miracle is Jesus' resurrection, which signifies a new creation and identity made possible in Christ. I think John is introducing us to a new creation—our new humanity—that can be rooted in Christ (i.e., a new identity). New Testament writers, like Paul, emphasize this new identity by repeating phrases like *in Christ*, *through Christ*, and *with Christ*.

This exercise is a simple way to have spiritual conversations about Jesus' mission and what it means to follow Him. Remember: Spiritual leadership invites us to be sensitive to God's light in the world. Raising kids is one way God is discipling us. And the end game of disciplemaking is spiritual reproduction. As parents animate faith, it allows kids to grow roots and begin to recognize the voice of the Good Shepherd.

A RHYTHM OF APPRENTICING

FINDING YOUR WINDOW:
MEALTIME, TRAVEL TIME, BEDTIME, AND MORNING TIME

> *Love the* LORD *your God with all your heart and with all your soul and with all your strength. These commandments that I give you today are to be on your hearts. Impress them on your children. Talk about them* **when you sit** *at home and* **when you walk** *along the road,* **when you lie down** *and* **when you get up.**
>
> DEUTERONOMY 6:5-7, *emphasis added*

"When you sit": At dinnertime, go around the table in two or three rounds, with each person saying one thing they're not good at and need help with during each round. The goal isn't fault-finding as much as it is creating emotional safety, offering relational transparency, and finding strength in confession.

"When you walk": As you drive, describe a recent conversation or reaction that you wish you could have handled differently. Offer an apology without justifying it. Ask for your child's forgiveness by inviting their consent: "Will you forgive me for . . . ?" Remember, God is discipling you as you disciple your kids. We lead by surrender and confession.

"When you lie down": At bedtime, ask each of your kids to say five things they're thankful for. If you're up for it, try to connect any of their responses to the names of God. For example, if you offer a prayer of thanks for your family pet or a friend down the street, connect that with how God is our Comforter. If it's for a grandparent, tie the prayer to God as our Provider. If it's for your house, explain how God is our Refuge, Strong Tower, and/or Hiding Place.

"When you get up": In the morning, think of two or three attributes of God you see in your kids and/or spouse. Take turns telling each other how you see Christ in the other person. The goal is to learn to speak to each other's potential. Help your kids and/or spouse see whom they can become in Christ.

DIY DISCIPLEMAKING ACTIVITY #1
Family Date Night

PLAN A FAMILY DATE NIGHT at a special location. Bring a few pre-planned prompts that allow everyone to speak blessings over one another. While sitting in a circle, choose a family member to focus on, and go around so that everyone has a chance to complete a sentence about that person. Give each family member a chance to hear what the rest of the family feels, sees, and loves about them. Here are some ideas for prompts:

- "The top ten things I love about you are . . ."
- "I love being home together because . . ."
- "Because of you, I am learning . . ."
- "I love you more than . . ."
- "_____ is just better when you're there."

CHAPTER 2

A RHYTHM FOR RENEWAL

Learning to Recognize and Respond to God's Voice

HAVE YOU EVER THOUGHT that the world God created isn't what He intended it to be? Jesus announced that the Kingdom of Heaven is at hand (Matthew 3:2), yet it's often hard to remember this when we encounter the extraordinary brokenness of the world in our daily lives. Parenting is a crucible where we operate out of sleep deprivation, a battle of wills, and both age-old and brand-new challenges.

Although it's hard to parent in this broken world, where we often make mistakes, Jesus' death makes it possible for anyone to get back up and begin again! Amid all the challenges, parenting is also a source of immeasurable joy that emanates from our all-in, love-till-it-hurts approach. Parenting can give us a glimpse of our Father's love toward us—but to see it, we need a rhythm to experience renewal.

Being saved means more than just believing you'll go to heaven when you die. Jesus announced that the Kingdom of Heaven is here *now*. What does that mean for you and me in our respective day-to-day realities as we juggle school pickups and extracurricular activities and navigate tough conversations with our kids? Sometimes we're just trying to make it through the day and the idea that renewal is possible for parents of children or teenagers might seem unattainable, even laughable. But renewal isn't simply recharging our batteries so we can live the life we want to live . . . because our lives aren't all about us. Christians experience renewal when we resensitize our hearts to recognize God's presence. This chapter explores how God seeks to redeem dark places and broken lives. Discovering a rhythm for renewal involves finding ways God invites us to return to Him. Renewal is about discerning signs of God's activity and helping our children see how the world can be as God intended. Along the way we discover how God disciples us as we disciple our kids.

LIGHT PEEKING THROUGH

There's no shortage of hole-in-the-wall clubs and bars lining Sixth Street in downtown Austin. Few cities can rival the concentration and quantity of live music venues there. Live music is the norm. It's *the* destination many a night for a primarily young-adult crowd. East Sixth has its own particular grime, reflecting a heavily trafficked college scene. On this night, it was South by Southwest (SXSW; a massive arts festival and conference), so all kinds of people—locals and tourists, troubadours and amateurs—were on hand. A stage is a stage, and at SXSW an audience can swell quickly. Standing in the back of a tiny club meant I was only about fifty feet from the stage. The room was full of bodies and enthusiasm. A-listers shoulder to shoulder with commoners gathered under the vibey banner of music appreciation. One after another, emerging talents stepped up in a musical carousel of sorts. The music felt as accessible as the artists themselves. While I was enjoying a sidebar conversation with friends, a lyric rang out above the bar chatter, interrupting me—

"The miracle is not walking on the water . . ." A soulful Black man was playing an acoustic guitar and belting it out like an anthem. The tiny club was hardly where I expected to be reminded of Sunday school stories, but the musician piqued my curiosity.

Again he sang, "The miracle is not walking on the water . . ." By this point, this singer had my undivided attention. I audibly asked, "What is it?" Right on cue, he answered, "The miracle is walking on the earth . . . day by day . . . step by step."[1]

It's been said that art imitates life. I especially love it when art *interrupts* life. This singer-songwriter, whom I came to know as Chris Pierce, reminded me that renewal is learning to find God in dark, stuck, and unexpected ways in ordinary places.

> *Renewal is learning to find God in dark, stuck, and unexpected ways in ordinary places.*

While your family context is far from a live show at a club at midnight, we are all searching for God's presence in the hard and the good, in the awe-inspiring and the ordinary, in our daily responsibilities and our spiritual deserts. The psalmist cries out like a parent desperately treading to keep their head above the waterline: "Where can I go from your Spirit? / Where can I flee from your presence? / If I go up to the heavens, you are there; / if I make my bed in the depths, you are there" (Psalm 139:7-8).

The miracle of our children isn't their birth or the legacy we hope to impart.

The miracle is what God does *in* and *through* us in parenting them—day by day, step by step.

Being a disciplemaker is more like being a tour guide than being a travel agent. We take the journey with our kids—through the dark, with fatigue, in uncertainty, searching for what's best while often battling our own gnawing insecurities. Nevertheless, God invites us as tour guides to point to the signs, smells, sounds, and tastes of God's presence.

Renewal is not what happens when we take a break from parenting; it's what God does in the middle of it.

Renewal is not what happens when we take a break from parenting; it's what God does in the middle of it.

CREATED FOR SABBATH

Sabbath has always been God's way of renewing us—but this kind of rest is not to be an end in itself. It's not about getting some "me time" to recharge our batteries and focus our energy on ourselves.

God's idea of Sabbath is that we *work from our rest*, not *rest from our work.*

We mostly get this backward in our society, which is why so many of us feel emotionally threadbare. We have calloused hearts, and we miss opportunities to experience prompts of God's Spirit. When we work from our rest, as God intended, we connect with God's Spirit and find strength, comfort, peace, and hope.

Sunday worship is historically associated with honoring the

Sabbath. Sunday is a day set apart for teaching of God's Word, sacramental worship, and embodied fellowship with an extended family of faith. In some instances, keeping the Sabbath means keeping a standing appointment for faith and community. In other cases, it can mean finding time to be quiet before God and drown out competing voices and false narratives. The ancient observance of the Sabbath was as much about trusting God with the demands and responsibilities of life as it was about worshiping God.

God seeks to be at the center of our hearts. And that requires constant recalibration, interruption of the relentless pursuit of survival and advancement touted in the West today.

My friend Morgan offered deep insight on the meaning of Sabbath rest: "It's not so much like a vacation but more like sleep. We can make it without a vacation, but we can't live without sleep."[2] Simply put, Sabbath is essential, not optional. The discipline isn't in resting as an escape from our work; the discipline is in prioritizing rest and preserving margins *so that* we can live and work with resensitized hearts, minds, and bodies. Renewal is not just the act of pursuing God, as if God is remaining at a distance. Morgan is discerning because he operates with a quiet center. It's not that he's not busy. He works with disadvantaged students at a university, supports aging parents daily, and is active in men's groups. Morgan finds God's presence as a prison ministry weekend volunteer as much as he did while teaching high school students for thirty years.

A rhythm for renewal helps us see what we have rather than what we lack. When we work from our rest, we remember who we are despite our shortcomings. We find our strength and worth *not* in winning or being right but in the Father's grace. When Jesus was questioned for healing on the Sabbath (which was forbidden by

Jewish law), He responded, "The Sabbath was made for man, not man for the Sabbath" (Mark 2:27). For the Sabbath to do what it was intended to do, we should understand how this rhythm is part of God's provision for us.

If we believe we are created for the Sabbath's sake, we will tend to

- follow rules to observe the day;
- experience more obligation than renewal; and
- conform rather than create, serve, worship, host, and celebrate.

In contrast, when we understand that the Sabbath is for *our* sake, we will

- understand that God has provided a way for us to abide with Him;
- trust God with our time, recognizing Him as the Source of our strength;
- discover a contribution beyond simply earning a living; and
- "work" at loving our neighbors and trusting God.

Making disciples without having a rhythm of renewal is like trying to operate a car without oil—it makes us seize. It's like baking bread and forgetting to add the yeast—nothing rises. Without a rhythm of renewal to cultivate sensitivity to God's activity in the world, we never get to appreciate the full extent of God's abundance, grace, pleasure, and presence.

When spiritually curious people attend church, their primary reason is to hear *about* God. That's a great first step, but it's not the end of their faith journeys. For those who have life-altering, habit-forming, Spirit-emanating relationships with Jesus, faith is fueled with the anticipation of hearing *from* God. As parent-disciplemakers we seek to reproduce a living faith in our kids, and prioritizing renewal is a subtle but formative way that our apprentices can observe the effect of God's Spirit and experience it for themselves.

RENEWAL AS RETURNING

A rhythm of renewal is not a phrase kids will use. I don't think I ever tried it out on my kids. Nevertheless, the practice provides a needed and fresh way to reimagine the critical biblical concept of repentance. When we hear that word, we typically think of our sins, inadequacies, and shortcomings. Yet true repentance is also a return to God's unwavering love. The Hebrew word for repentance (*teshuvah*) refers to a turning. It's the idea that we renew our faith, our human strength, and the relationships we hold most dear when we respond to the prompts of God's Spirit. Parents who seek to do right by their kids and raise them to know the love of Jesus need a daily reminder:
Our Lord is closer than you think.
And you are likely more capable than you realize.
Seriously. I'm convinced that's how God sees each of us. At the outset of His public ministry, Jesus boldly announced the present availability of the Kingdom of Heaven. In other words, it's not just a future destination for believers. We can experience and access heaven . . . on earth!

> "The time has come," [Jesus] said. "The kingdom of God has come near. Repent and believe the good news!"
> MARK 1:15

Three segments of this verse show us how we can help advance the Kingdom of Heaven here on earth:

- **Segment #1: "The time has come."** As we live in a broken world and deal with our need-to-grow areas, God seeks to interrupt the darkness around us and within us. In the original language of the Gospel of Mark, the word translated "time" in "the time has come" is not *chronos*, a word we may find familiar since it's the root of our word *chronology*. *Chronos* often describes measured time But Mark intead employs *kairos*, which also denotes the concept of time but often refers more to an opportunity than to a scheduled event.

    Time is in short supply for parents and is therefore a treasured commodity. We don't usually like to stop for what we haven't planned for, whether it's a sibling argument in the church parking lot or a red traffic light when we're already running late. We can be hostile to whatever feels like a waste of time. We worry that we don't have enough time, that we must squeeze everything we possibly can out of every single moment to function in our fast-moving society. But God, who is outside time, is in the things that interrupt us as much as He is in the things we plan for. God often uses interruptions to teach us about curiosity, wonder, and imagination. Children tend to be more practiced at living in the moment than the average adult and therefore more willing to welcome the unexpected. Maybe we can learn from our kids how to yield to opportunities rather than be ruled by our schedules. What initially seems like an interruption might just be an invitation to a heaven-on-earth encounter.

+ **Segment #2: "The kingdom of God has come near."** Too often, we think of heaven as a reward we won't experience until we die. As a result, we live our lives as if heaven is far off. But in Mark 1:15 Jesus describes it as near, present, and at hand! And He suggests that we need a childlike faith if we want to discover the Kingdom here and now. Kids are never in a hurry, are prone to wonder (and wander), are curious about everything, and always have time for interruptions. If we pay attention, kids can help us recognize God's voice and presence. If you have young children, intentionally walk at their slower pace for a while, trying to be more still, attentive, and/or sensitive to signs of the Kingdom as you do. See how God might offer you a dose of joy.

+ **Segment #3: "Repent and believe the good news!"** Since believers are invited to be agents of hope, God also gives us agency to participate in renewing the world, beginning with our hearts. Repentance typically elicits feelings of inadequacy and shame. Jesus' invitation isn't to dwell endlessly on our sins and shortcomings but rather to examine our hearts, reconsider our course, and turn toward or away from something. Frequently, God's Spirit speaks through a personal hesitation or a "check" in our spirits. We want to pay attention to these nudges and consider, *Am I being asked to turn away from sin, resentment, slander, fear, or perfectionism? Am I invited to turn toward compassion, patience, forgiveness, or generosity?*

The more sensitive our hearts are before God, the greater our awareness of God's presence. This is as personal as it gets with the God of creation! While God's Spirit does convict and lead us, He doesn't shame or guilt-trip us into obedience. We become sensitive to a first impression or initial reaction as we examine events, circumstances, and conversations, asking ourselves questions like *What does Scripture say about this? Do I need to confess something? Whom can I talk to about this? Is there a pattern, or is this connected to other events?* Ultimately, we're trying to figure out what God is saying and what we should do in response.

REMEMBERING WHO YOU ARE

If a rhythm of renewal is learning to turn and re-turn, then we must be returning *to* something. In fourth grade, Bjørn was playing with three neighbor boys in the woods. There was a creek with some rocks that formed a dam. All the boys were wielding sticks, and as Bjørn pried at a rock with his, he accidentally splashed the boy next to him. The neighbor boy responded by striking Bjørn in the face with his stick. Being a peacemaker, Bjørn's only response was to apologize for splashing. Later, the same kid yelled at him for something else petty. After I heard about this incident, a simmering anger lingered in me for the next couple of days.

I kept revisiting the conversation with Bjørn to help him learn how to stick up for himself and make sure he understood what a healthy friendship looks like. I kept pushing him to have boundaries so it wouldn't happen again. The boy called the next day and apologized because his mom made him (I don't know how she found out). Even though the stick episode hurt him, Bjørn didn't want to make a big deal out of it. As a parent, it's hard for me to watch our kids be not just mistreated but also hurt and disappointed. As I stewed over this situation, I remember Annika saying (seemingly out of nowhere), "You're a good dad." I certainly didn't feel like a good dad in the moment, so I asked why she would say that. "Because you care so much about what happens to us and you always want the best for us," Annika replied. There

I was thinking I'd failed to protect my son. And there, in His wisdom, the Father spoke this divine affirmation over me.

God sees, grieves, and delights with us.

Identity is about who we are—not about what we do or fail to do. Identity is also a narrative. As children of God, the arcs of our stories bend to reveal God's plot in creation. The most important thing we can understand is our story in light of God's redemptive story.

At the beginning of Jesus' public ministry, He left Galilee for the Jordan River. John the Baptist was there, drawing crowds as he invited the people of God to repent and be baptized. Upon Jesus' immersion, we read in Luke's Gospel,

> Heaven was opened and the Holy Spirit descended on him in bodily form like a dove. And a voice came from heaven: "You are my Son, whom I love; with you I am well pleased."
> LUKE 3:21-22

As I studied this passage recently, something occurred to me that I hadn't thought of before. Before Jesus had healed or fed anyone; before Jesus had taught one lesson, saved one soul, or done anything to build a résumé worthy of being the Messiah; before Jesus could make Himself more lovable or worthy of God's affection, He received a divine affirmation. This statement is ground zero for how we might find our worth and acceptance and, as disciples, put the divine on display.

Is there anything our kids can do to make us love them more? We may not like everything they say and do, but does their behavior ever call our love into question? Now think about how God views us. He knows our blind spots and sees our earnest desires, honest efforts, and careless shortcomings. But that knowledge doesn't change the nature of our relationship with Him. The apostle Paul addressed people as saints, not sinners. He called himself the chief of sinners (1 Timothy 1:15, KJV) but also said he wasn't who he once was (1 Timothy 1:12-13). When we are firmly grounded in Christ—as new creations—we can deal with our sins because our identity and belonging are not in question. Renewal invites us to return to this divine affirmation as our hearts' home.

FRUIT > RESULTS

Some people think God is looking for results, but Scripture tells us He's looking for fruit.[3] The difference is that results are what happen *around* us; fruit is what happens *inside* us. How might we disciple our kids to recognize and respond to God's voice?

Practicing renewal is how we exercise faith as a muscle. We get stronger while becoming more sensitive to the needs and opportunities around us.

Admittedly, parenting feels like one interruption after another. But to the extent we can discern and turn toward a need, problem, or opportunity in the moment, our kids notice how God's presence and desires can animate our ordinary lives. If we rarely mention God in conversation with our kids, how will they know He's on our minds? Our relationships with Christ are personal, but we can't treat them as private and hope that our kids will discern His voice on their own.

Our pasts only describe who we were, which is different from defining who we are and who we will become. The New Testament writers announced that who we are in Christ is our identity: We are each a "new creation" (2 Corinthians 5:17), which means that in Christ, we're restored, reconciled, and righteous.

These writers understood that if believers kept learning who they were in Christ, they would know (or at least figure out) what to do. Trusting God is more than just praying that something bad doesn't happen. Practicing renewal is how we exercise faith as a muscle. We get stronger while becoming more sensitive to the needs and opportunities around us.

PRAYING WITH PRESENCE

Parents don't have much opportunity for silence, spiritual or otherwise. But even amid activity and noise, renewal creates in us a growing awareness of God's presence. If that sounds impossible or unrelatable, that's fair. I get how it feels. Apprenticing under Christ and in the Spirit takes time. The process can feel more subtle than grand.

The next time you find yourself feeling rushed or threadbare while preparing an unremarkable dinner that you know won't be appreciated . . .

 . . . and you spy a pile of laundry left undone . . .

 . . . while you hear kids bickering . . .

 . . . then realize the dog hasn't been fed today . . .

 . . . before your spouse tells you they need to leave tomorrow morning on a last-minute business trip . . .

 . . . and it occurs to you that you're still in your morning workout clothes and forgot to brush your teeth today . . .

in that moment, imagine that God is present in the room with you. He sees this once-good-now-chaotic creation.

In the same way you deeply love your family and long to see them flourish, God also sees and loves the mess of our humanity.

He longs—as you do—for something more. The world God created is not as He intended it to be.

It's not ideal, not sustainable, *and* not the end of the story. God is present in all of it!

He aches, yearns, grieves, provides, and abides as the longing, loving parent He is. God sent His Son into the world, and He also sends each of us to enliven His presence through the Holy Spirit. As we learn to discover the incarnational presence and care of the Father in our messy lives, we find subtle strength, poise, and hope. As you and I sense God's presence, we can experience grace in unideal places.

I remember making a conscious shift in prayer. Before I started praying with presence, I had God in mind, but I often prayed as if no one were present.

The Unseen can feel like absence, like we're requesting wish fulfillment from the sky.

But I started praying as if God were present with me in the here and now. You can call it mental gymnastics, but it made a difference in my prayers.

Praying with presence felt more personal and conversational, like meeting a dear friend over coffee, with as much listening as sharing.

It also had a way of nurturing conviction, like if I was feeling grumpy or impatient or when I could see God's presence affecting my feelings of envy.

And I experienced contentment and gratitude.

Rethinking my prayer life has helped me sense God in real time, not just in retrospect, where I wish I could've handled things differently. I still find myself, at times, acting just like the crowds following Jesus who asked for more signs: "What sign then will you give that we may see it and believe you? What will you do?" (John 6:30). But prayer is less about achieving tangible results than about growing closer to God. It turns our gaze to God, to His concern for the world, and to our participation in its restoration.

WHOLEHEARTEDNESS

I've heard the "frog in the kettle" story for years. It's the one about someone putting a frog in a pot and as the water warms and begins to boil, the frog fails to realize the gradual temperature change and eventually gets cooked. This story is meant to warn us that we are all susceptible to being destroyed by gradual changes because we don't notice them. Psychologist Adam Grant investigated the story's origins and found that it doesn't hold up. A frog will jump out of a pot as soon as the water gets too warm. Grant's clever point is this: "It's not the frogs who fail to reevaluate. It's us."[4]

Many parents fall victim to the familiar no-margins parenting story—the one that tells us we need to give our kids every advantage to help them succeed, keep them active and engaged so their development progresses optimally, and give them everything we never had growing up. Most parents can't avoid some measure of squeeze, but we need to be careful not to let it consume us.

This is where a rhythm of renewal comes into play. A rhythm of renewal will give parents the frog-like sensitivity to know when the heat of your family priorities and personal commitments is boiling the Spirit-filled life out of you!

In seventh grade at spring baseball tournament weekend, Bjørn took an inside pitch off his hands while batting and broke his thumb. It ended his season and took him out of his last middle school golf team tournaments. Initial disappointment quickly gave way to enjoyment as we had more family dinners, game nights, and frozen yogurt outings. We spent the next few weekends reading, watching movies together, doing yard work, and swimming. It's amazing how renewing it can be to spend quality time relaxing with your family.

I am reminded of the apostle Paul. Here was a guy on a mission. After his dramatic conversion, there was no stopping his missionary travels, church planting, and future-leader mentoring, all while he was trying to live down his checkered past. And although God was probably glad Paul was now operating as an ambassador for the Kingdom instead of against it, God had more in mind for Paul—slow down long enough to write! Instead of just telling Paul to slow down, God allowed him to experience several rounds of imprisonment. I'm suspicious that's the only way God could get Paul to slow down long enough to do the significant work of leaving a legacy. During those times in chains, Paul penned at least four letters that we know as, aptly, the Prison Epistles. Ephesians, Philippians, Colossians, and Philemon were all written while Paul was locked up. What a productive alternative to the pace and work he'd been keeping. It's inspiring and comforting how God can redeem any condition, even our Kingdom contributions from the margins.

Once again, I think family is God's principal laboratory on earth for children of God to experience His presence and grace. It's also the way for us to experiment with reproducing a living faith into our children's hearts. In my family's case, we needed the interruption of a broken thumb. I know there are many good activities for your kids to be involved in. But to those of us in the West with lots of ambition and undiagnosed FOMO that might cause our kids not to excel or be included or prepared, we're too quick to sacrifice our relational, financial, physical, and spiritual margins. Exhaustion is not just a matter of physical, emotional, or mental fatigue. It can have a dulling effect on a spiritual level too. *Exhaustion is not only a loss of care but also a limitation of how much care we can express.* The lesson here? Less is more. Jesus said the Kingdom is about abundant life (John 10:10). As we see signs of scarcity in the margins of our cities, God invites us to be ambassadors of heaven. Discipling our kids means awakening them to how we might follow God wholeheartedly.

Wholeheartedness starts to feel impossible when we realize how deeply we care. Instead of preparing our kids for the journey, we often try to prepare the road for our kids. We are tempted to act as lawn mower parents so the path will be as easy, convenient, and enjoyable as possible, forgetting that our kids need to learn to journey on unhewn paths to be ready for consequences in the real world.

We care greatly about our kids' success in every area of life.

We care deeply about our aging parents.

We care about our economic security and maximizing our enjoyment of weekends and holidays.

We care about health, debt, education, the economy, democracy, freedom, injustice, quality friendships, and those on the margins.

We spend so much time at the limits of our care that it's exhausting. It's hard to respond to one more thing when you're struggling with compassion fatigue.

In each season of life, it's hard to see how thick it is when you're in the thick of it. Adrenaline, stress, pressure, and constant motion desensitize all of us. Yet God seeks to awaken us so we know Him not from a distance but rather as a Friend whose lap, shoulder, and hand feel readily accessible.

PARENTS POINTING TO THE SIGNS OF THE KINGDOM

One of the things I love about Jesus' teaching ministry is that He didn't prepare sermon outlines or write stuffy books. Instead, He simply found object lessons from daily life to illustrate God's activity in the world.[5] The disciples were in proximity to these opportunistic moments. Tender Kingdom conversations often unfold without a plan. We can be looking for opportune moments to teach our children even while we run errands, do laundry, or help with homework.

Three weeks after fifteen-year-old Bjørn and Clara started dating, he and I played a memorable round of golf together. It wasn't our scorecards I remember but the conversation that unfolded as we played.

"Bjørn, I want to talk to you about Clara."

"Dad, please, no. Mom just talked to me about boundaries."

I laughed at his reaction to the prospect of another awkward conversation. "That's funny," I responded, "but that's not where I was going. My question is: Do you think you'll marry Clara?"

Bjørn rolled his eyes, gave me a don't-be-ridiculous look, and said, "Dad, c'mon . . ."

It was the obvious reaction I sought, but I wanted Bjørn to say it out loud.

I replied, "You're probably right. Most people don't end up at the altar with their first girlfriend or boyfriend. That's not the point. I'm happy for you because Clara seems like a great girl to get to know. I'm excited about how much dating can teach you about yourself. You get to figure out the kind of person you want to be, to decide if you like who you are when you're with the other person. It's common for a person to lose themself in a relationship, but that's not healthy for either person. God has so much to teach us when our hearts get involved with new feelings of attraction. So it's really important to think about this: *You might be dating someone else's future wife.* Even if you two only date for a short time, you need to be very thoughtful in how you treat her, how you speak to her, and how you touch her."

Bjørn sat in the golf cart, staring out at a fairway.

"Dad, I don't think you understand how often all the high school guys talk about what they do with girls."

"Well, buddy . . . I have some idea, and as a dad who also has a daughter, it saddens and concerns me."

After giving him a moment for reflection, I said, "And Bjørn?

Don't you wish there were a dad somewhere having this same conversation with his son because that kid is dating *your* future wife?"

The Bible isn't a textbook from which we derive rules. I didn't give my son strict dos and don'ts, but I encouraged sensitivity in caring for one of God's beloved daughters. Scripture reveals what is true about God and tells the redemptive story of Him remaking the world as He intended in the Garden. Scripture is a wonderful source of wisdom, which isn't the same thing as a rule book.

Disciplemaking is pointing our kids to signs of what heaven on earth looks like. I didn't plan to have this conversation or schedule this tee time to talk about dating. I'd never been asked these questions myself at Bjørn's age. I simply tried to combine common sense with the Spirit's guidance and point Bjørn to God's heart. All I hoped to do was help him see what God's heart might be for him and his girlfriend.

While discipling Timothy, Paul wrote to his young apprentice:

> As for you, continue in what you have learned and have become convinced of, because you know those from whom you learned it, and how from infancy you have known the Holy Scriptures, which are able to make you wise for salvation through faith in Christ Jesus. All Scripture is God-breathed and is useful for teaching, rebuking, correcting and training in righteousness, so that the servant of God may be thoroughly equipped for every good work.
> 2 TIMOTHY 3:14-17

The critical disciplemaking charge is how we might nurture sensitivity to God's Spirit and reorient our kids' lives around His Kingdom. What's fun about this story is that, after going to separate colleges and continuing to date for seven years, Bjørn and Clara later walked down the aisle and said, "I do."

FINDING YOUR RHYTHM: SEEKING THE KINGDOM

Take a few evenings at dinner or bedtime to read a parable or two where Jesus describes the Kingdom of God. Host a conversation about what He means. Keep in mind that Jesus is painting a picture of heaven on earth. Think of heaven on earth as the world God intended, not the broken one we know.

- Matthew 13:24-30 . . . like a man who sowed good seed in his field of wheat
- Matthew 13:31-35 . . . like a mustard seed, like yeast
- Matthew 13:44-46 . . . like hidden treasure, like a merchant looking for fine pearls
- Matthew 18:1-4 . . . like a child
- Matthew 18:21-35 . . . like a merciful master
- Matthew 20:1-16 . . . like a generous landowner
- Matthew 22:1-10 . . . like a king who prepared a wedding feast
- Mark 4:26-29 . . . like growing seed
- Luke 13:20-21 . . . like yeast

After reading each of the passages, ask your children these two questions, and engage with their responses:

1. What does Jesus want us to understand about heaven by using this image?
2. If Jesus wants us to understand what heaven is like, how does He want us to act on earth?

FINDING YOUR WINDOW:
MEALTIME, TRAVEL TIME, BEDTIME, AND MORNING TIME

> *Love the* LORD *your God with all your heart and with all your soul and with all your strength. These commandments that I give you today are to be on your hearts. Impress them on your children. Talk about them* **when you sit** *at home and* **when you walk** *along the road,* **when you lie down** *and* **when you get up.**
>
> DEUTERONOMY 6:5-7, *emphasis added*

"When you sit": At dinnertime, try praying before and after the meal, imagining that Jesus is physically present at the table with you. You might even add another chair to illustrate His presence. See if or how the prayers might sound different. Just as Jesus is with you, pray for ways to be with and for others. Give thanks and pray for the farmers who grew your produce, the ranchers who raised the livestock, the people who transported, bought, and sold the food, and those who stocked the shelves. How might each of these people benefit from your prayers, God's provision, and His presence?

"When you walk": During your car rides, ask kids to keep devices off. Share how you notice God's presence in a need that's not your own, or describe an interruption that you felt God was part of.

"When you lie down": At bedtime, describe a recent conversation or reaction you wish you could have handled differently—maybe an impatient overreaction toward your child or an ugly moment in traffic they witnessed your reaction to. Is there a recent encounter you could make amends for? Choose to find God's strength in vulnerability.

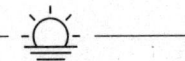

"When you get up": In the morning, remind your kids of who they are in Christ. Use a verse from Paul. For example: God sees them as saints (Ephesians 1:18). They're God's workmanship or masterpiece (Ephesians 2:10). They're not alone (Hebrews 13:5). They are citizens of heaven (Philippians 3:20), are "hidden with Christ in God" (Colossians 3:3), have the "mind of Christ" (1 Corinthians 2:16), and are "the righteousness of God" (2 Corinthians 5:21). Speak God's truth over them!

DIY DISCIPLEMAKING ACTIVITY #2
Renewal Awards

HOST A FAMILY WATCH PARTY of Pixar's movie *Up*.

After his wife's death, Carl feels like his story is done. But Ellie always intended for him to continue his adventure. To Ellie, life was always an adventure, even when there were setbacks, disappointments, and losses. Carl turns the page of Ellie's photo album and gains a brand-new perspective.

In a similar way, the measure of a disciple's growth is a growing ability to see what God sees. *Up* offers a perspective of heaven as here and now instead of then and later, which is exactly the kind of life God invites us into.

For this activity, collect a dozen bottle caps, a glue gun, and a ribbon to make bottle cap badges of your own.

- According to Carl, the "Ellie Badge" is the "highest honor [he] can bestow."[6] Tell your kids, "Here's how you help me see what God sees . . ."

- Explain how you're learning about God's love, patience, grace, and kindness because of something they've shown you. I'm confident everyone's spirits will go up!

✽ Ask your kids if they want to make badges for any of their friends, relatives, neighbors, or extended faith-family members. It's never too early for them to begin to learn how to see glimpses of God in the people around them.

Note: If your kids are preteens, "too old," or "too cool" (especially the boys) and not into crafting, just invite them to join you around the craft table. Make a badge and speak a perspective-changing blessing over them. See if that homemade badge finds a place in their room.

CHAPTER 3

A RHYTHM OF HOSPITALITY

Making Room for New Faces in New Places

THE LONG LUNCH TABLE where I sat with my daughter, Annika, was separated mainly by second graders of opposite genders. Across from us were two girls having a curious exchange. "Are you Christian or Jewish?" one girl asked assertively. An unassuming girl with square glasses sliding down her nose peered back over the top of the frames with a shrug of her shoulders.

"Uh, I dunno."

"Well, do you believe in God?"

"Sure," she replied. The first responded conclusively, "Then you're a Christian, like me!"

I hesitated, thinking, *Do I need to jump in on this one?* I took a breath . . . and stopped. Instead of explaining the finer points of atonement theory and God's love in sending Jesus to these young girls on a public-school campus, I bit my tongue.

Later that afternoon, I was stuck in traffic with ten-year-old Bjørn. I told him my lunchtime story of the two girls. He laughed (though I'm unsure whether he was laughing at the girls or me). Thinking I had a good teaching moment on my hands, I asked, "What do you think it means to be a Christian?"

Bjørn's first response was to look up, put his head on the headrest, and say, "Dad, you ask this question all the time!" Now, I had to laugh at myself and apologize (I tend to have difficulty remembering which thoughts I've spoken aloud and which I've kept to myself). But my most earnest desire for my kids—and maybe this is your prayer too—is that they might know God in a personal, orienting way.

The reality is that asking a group of adult believers "What does it mean to be a Christian?" would probably yield a hundred different answers. We all have different ideas about what faith looks like and which aspects are most important. If adults struggle to articulate what it means to be Christian, it's easy to see how children would too.

I resonate with musician Nick Cave in the book *Faith, Hope and Carnage* where he explains why he prefers the term *religious* over *spiritual*. He says, "Spirituality . . . can mean almost anything. . . . [but religion] makes demands on us. For me, it involves some wrestling with the idea of faith."[1] And the demand of the Christian religion is that you become people of love.

Being a disciple of Jesus goes beyond believing the words He spoke to believing that He is the embodiment of God and living out of that truth. Salvation isn't about adopting the right beliefs now and going to heaven when we die. It's about discovering that we're created in the image of God and that we belong to God. You've likely heard of the Incarnation, the theological concept that God took on the form of a human and "made his dwelling among us," as John puts it in his Gospel (John 1:14). We can also incarnate the love of God by showing that our faith is accessible and inviting to all.

In this chapter, I want to unpack the concept of hospitality, which makes the gospel good news for life on earth. Hospitality can involve opening your home, yes, but it's also much more: It's about helping you find the words for the hope you have (see 1 Peter 3:15). And I explore ways to make Christ known to our kids, where we live, through our vocations, and with those God gives us favor and influence with.

FROM BELIEVING TO BELONGING

Hospitality allows parents to discover their greatest Kingdom contribution while encountering God with their hearts on the line.

Simply acknowledging or even believing there's a God is not good news. The main Hebrew word for "knowing" (*yada*[2]) is primarily relational—it's not simply a cognitive knowing. It's about being known, not just knowing about something. I want our children to have the kind of faith that's more than a feeling and can rise above circumstances. I want them to see their lives as "hidden with Christ" (Colossians 3:3) yet imagine ways to be part of God's hospitality, of restoring heaven on earth.

Hospitality is a helpful metaphor for salvation because it makes a significant statement about our need to feel like we belong. Imagine if one of your kids didn't feel like they belonged in your family. You'd do everything you could to help them understand that they're a vital part of it. Now imagine how our heavenly Father feels when we don't feel lovable, accepted, and treasured . . . and what lengths He'll go to to help us realize how much He loves us.

As a dad who raised teenagers, I was amazed to learn that in ancient Israel, at around fifteen years old, Jewish boys at the top of their class would approach a rabbi and ask "Can I follow you?"

Essentially, they were inquiring, "Do I have what it takes to be like you?" If their request was declined, they'd return to their family trade. It's important to note that Jesus reversed this cultural norm by inviting the disciples—each of whom was already working in a trade—to "come, follow me" (Matthew 4:19). Essentially, Jesus was telling them, "You already have what it takes to be like Me." And the same is true for all believers. This is good news for any parent who lacks confidence or feels unqualified to be a spiritual leader at home.

Family is about belonging without trying.

Family provides identity—who we are—without our having to earn it.

Family offers a shared likeness that can give glimpses of what God is like.

A rhythm of hospitality sets the table for God's family to access heaven on earth. It opens the door for belonging. It feasts on a new identity as it shapes a new appetite for God's reconciliation and restoration in increasing ways, even if we're still learning to host! People more than programs reproduce the incarnational life of Christ. And parents—with the Spirit's help and alongside a faith community—get to do this handcrafting.

GOD WITH US, WITH OTHERS

With only a night-light on, Annika in bed, and me kneeling at her side, I saw a glimpse of the divine in the ordinary. It was common for us to pray together for friends in our church. I would share with my kids how God had given me the influence to be a trusted voice for people struggling even though I couldn't fix their problems. On this night, we prayed for Miss Carrie and Mr. Noah, a couple in our church.[3] Annika remembered our times with their family. Sadly, it appeared like they were headed for a divorce. I hadn't divulged any confidential details or anything about their personal stories. Annika just knew that their family needed prayer.

As we sat in pj's in the dimly lit room about to start praying, she asked, "Daddy, did Miss Carrie have a hard life growing up, or did something happen to her?"

I had to pause before responding. I was as shocked as you'd be by someone reading your mail. Though she was only eight years old, Annika had enough insight to ask about the deeper meaning behind someone's tough situation. Without going into detail, I offered, "Yeah, Annika, she had a hard life growing up. Her home became an unsafe place for her. In high school, she had to go live with a new family."

The truth was that Carrie's mom had abandoned her as a little girl and she'd been raised by an alcoholic, abusive stepfather. When she came to school with two black eyes at age sixteen, Carrie was removed from that house. But no one ever effectively cared for her emotionally. Noah was a good man who provided well for her and the kids but seemed emotionally inattentive. He was kind but didn't seem to know how to help her feel loved, heard, safe, or cared for.

After praying for Noah and Carrie that night, Annika's insight into their plight lingered in my mind. This is the kind of sensitivity disciples seek to cultivate. We try to see past the circumstances and symptoms to the underlying needs and pain. It's easy to dismiss my daughter's question as that of a tenderhearted child who's naturally empathetic. On the other hand, you could speculate that God's Spirit was nurturing a gift of discernment in her. As her dad, I had the privilege of witnessing and helping cultivate her gift. I received Annika's insight as a gracious nudge to resist the temptation to let my heart become calloused.

I couldn't help but think of how God met Hagar, a runaway

servant girl, in the desert. Just like Carrie, she was running from an abusive situation. As a servant and a woman in a society where both were at the bottom of the caste system, Hagar likely hadn't felt truly seen—acknowledged as a human made in God's image—by anyone before. That changed when the angel of the Lord met her. After their desert interview, Hagar says, "You are the God who sees me" (Genesis 16:13). This is where we encounter the name El Roi, "The God Who Sees," in Scripture, and it's revealing. Sometimes we miss the presence of God. He is trying to care for us, but our pace or the emotional weight we're carrying might be making it hard to perceive. It's common to have a hard time noticing, much less receiving, God's care and provision. Yet even when we're too wrapped up in our own affairs to discern His presence, God—El Roi—sees us. God asks Hagar two questions: "Where have you come from, and where are you going?" (Genesis 16:8). These two questions can help every disciple find a rhythm for hospitality. Everyone we meet has a past that informs their present. And by offering Christian hospitality, we might just influence their need to heal, trust, forgive, or be courted by the Spirit to know the love of the Father.

Nowhere is a rhythm of hospitality more natural than in our own homes. As parents, we hold unparalleled influence over our children. Imagine how our kids can be impacted by observing Mom's and Dad's sensitivity to the prompts of God's Spirit. Speaking metaphorically:

Hospitality often has a taste.

It typically has a feel.

There's usually a scent to discern and experience alongside God's presence.

The Spirit stirs beyond the seen and physical realm, and our senses can pick up on traces of Him. The more we practice hospitality, the easier it becomes to sense God's presence. Sometimes hospitality is our ability to make room for another—a friend, a stranger, a neighbor, a child, the least of these. Other times, hospitality is our ability to receive counsel, kindness, favor, or help from another (often an unexpected source).

HIDDEN IN PLAIN SIGHT

A new phase of Jesus' ministry began when He sent out the apostles to do the type of preaching, teaching, and healing that they had observed Him doing (Luke 10:1-20). This was the third tour of Galilee by Jesus and His disciples. On the first tour, Jesus had traveled with the four fishermen. On the second, the Twelve had been with Him. On the third, Jesus traveled alone after sending out the seventy-two two by two. In so doing, He previewed the great commission, which would come after His resurrection. He wanted to teach His disciples about evangelism, and He did this by teaching them about hospitality. No longer would the disciples simply gather in the Temple or stay within the comfort of their small group. Now they were to share what they'd learned from their rabbi. Jesus gave the seventy-two power and authority and encouraged them to find people of peace—people who are kind and receptive, offering them meals, housing, and work.

When Jesus sent the seventy-two, He told them to take nothing with them for the journey. Instead, they were to rely on the hospitality and favor of strangers. When it comes to using our faith for good, often the best thing we can do is let someone care for us in unexpected ways. When we do, two things happen: *God provides for us. And God draws people together.*

Think about it: When we feel most alive, we find ways to contribute. We discover our deepest connection in relationships when we find ways to personally serve others, to give of ourselves.

A person who resists offers of assistance or acts of kindness might be inadvertently turning away the ability to become closer to the person offering help.

Imagine your child wants to spend their birthday money on treating you to your favorite Starbucks drink. It's natural to see that as unnecessary. (After all, it's their birthday!) Yet by resisting your child's generous and sacrificial desire, you might rob them of the blessing of expressing their tangible love and drawing near to you. What about saying yes to that drink and telling people about how much you enjoyed it? What about highlighting the generosity with which it was given and with each sip describing it as tasting better than any other drink because it was offered with love? Whether it be from our children, someone with lesser means, or even a stranger, we acknowledge God as the Source of our lives by receiving help, simple gestures, and small acts of kindness.

Hospitality is about helping others feel seen just as God sees us. It's about allowing people to feel heard the same way God hears us.

We make room for God by receiving others.

Hospitality is about helping others feel seen just as God sees us.

It's about allowing people to feel heard the same way God hears us.

As parents who operate simultaneously as disciples and apprentices, we make ourselves available, even interruptible. Sometimes that means hosting people who might never return the invitation. Other times it's allowing people to bless us. In either case, we're invited to bear witness even when we lack time or words. As we make room for others, our kids learn how God makes room for us. If you still feel apprehensive about teaching your kids to practice hospitality, the good news is this: Christ is already at work in you and others, paving the way.

Imagine how amazing it would be—what a testimony—if our

children could see how God is active in the world by preparing people in advance for us to bless and be blessed by. Guess what? He does!

Faith is not something we just revert to when we feel helpless.

Faith grows as we trust and believe God will intervene and respond.

As our kids observe us engaging with seemingly random people in need, the more a practice of hospitality makes sense. We're not looking for our kids to evangelize strangers but rather to imagine how their faith might deepen as they witness Mom and Dad identifying people of peace. This is where faith is more art than science, more caught than taught.

Disciplemaking isn't about having the perfect approach or all the right answers or even about being convincing. It's about learning whom the Spirit has prepared for us and both offering and receiving God's provision. According to Scripture, we all appear to have people of peace in our lives. It's also safe to assume each of us is someone else's person of peace. How we give *and* receive reveals God.

REFRAMING SALVATION

I once took an unusual FaceTime call from a single mom. We'd been introduced two years earlier by friends who knew of my and Laurel's experience with four miscarriages. Maria had immigrated with her husband and son to grow their family in the States.[4] A miscarriage had led to a separation, which had led to him starting another family. This mom's pain ran as deep as her contempt for God. Her surprising call was to tell me about her recent encounter with God.

"I was trimming my rosebushes in my backyard. The neighbors were also working in their yard while a radio program played on the other side of a six-foot-high fence. They went back inside but left the radio on. I sat with my knees in the dirt, hearing someone speak about God . . . and I couldn't stop listening! David, it felt like someone was trying to give me a hug . . . but I couldn't receive it! David . . . I don't want to be hurt anymore. I don't want to be mad anymore, but I don't know what to do!"

Only God could have brought together two strangers from different cultures, initially to share their pain, doubt, and anger over their respective losses, to eventually bring redemption through a friendship centered in hope in God. This is the embodiment of good news! Hospitality is a way to increasingly experience the gospel as good news. I graciously listened, encouraged Maria, prayed for her, and invited her into a community of faith.

Hospitality makes Christ accessible to road-weary pilgrims needing hope, help, and healing. Traditionally, the church has talked about "evangelism," "sharing your faith," and "witnessing." This language causes many of us to squirm. Instead of sharing a convincing argument, what if we articulate what Jesus' Good News means to us personally?

When Jesus encountered the Samaritan woman at the well, He showed hospitality (John 4:1-42). Jesus didn't condemn her or remind her of sound doctrine. Jesus made the Kingdom of God accessible, gracious, and healing. In hosting a conversation at the well, Jesus offered dignity to a person with a reputation, one who was left to draw water by herself in the heat of the day. He valued her because she, like all of us, bore the image of God.

If we want to teach our kids about who God is, we shouldn't start with who they aren't—with everything they're doing wrong. If people figure out who they are, they figure out how to live. As we discover how we're made in God's image, we find ways to animate His likeness through us in our ordinary daily lives.

As a pastor, I've had to unlearn certain things in order to grow. Early on, I was trained to share a plan of salvation using the Romans Road,[5] which begins with "All have sinned and fall short of the glory of God" (Romans 3:23). But here's the thing: If we begin a plan for salvation here, what our kids can easily misunderstand is that God has set an unreachable moral bar for us. It's decidedly *not* good news nor a great way to be human if behavior is the most important thing. It doesn't effectively communicate a God who's hospitable, inviting, gracious, and loving. Sadly, many adult Christians have never outgrown this understanding. People commonly signal spiritual resignation by saying, "Well, I'm just a sinner saved by grace." The problem is that God doesn't see us that way. Astonishingly, He sees it through the righteousness of Christ (see 1 Corinthians 1:30; Philippians 1:11; 3:9)!

When we inevitably fall short, we fail to reflect God's image to the world.

But that doesn't disqualify us from God's love!

God sent His Son as part of the larger story of His covenant family and redeeming love for His creation. No parent wants their child to grow up thinking they're never good enough; why would our heavenly Father feel any different?

The whole point of the Bible is *not* merely to answer the question *How can I save my soul so I can go to heaven when I die?*[6]

The Bible is about God coming down to earth to be with His people.

God wanted to do that from the beginning. We see this in what He did in Jesus and in what He does through the Holy Spirit now. This is the Kingdom of Heaven on earth: Eternity has already begun! The gospel is not about evacuating this broken place called earth but about bringing heaven and earth together as a renewed and restored creation. This was the vision in the Garden. God has promised to return and restore all things (Acts 3:20-21). But in the present time, God longs to reconcile with humanity (through Jesus) so we can be part of His redeeming work. Salvation reveals that we belong because we've been created in the image of God.

HOSPITALITY AS BEARING WITNESS

My friend and mentor Leonard Sweet explains how hospitality plays a part in homegrown disciplemaking from our children's infancy:

> As parents, giving our children the freedom to choose their faith is like telling them to choose their language. At birth, parents naturally choose their children's verbal language. At baptism, parents choose their children's faith language. When children are born into a family, they learn the family name, identity, traditions, practices, life line, and character. Shared stories and songs create collective identities.[7]

As parents, hospitality means we embody Christ for our kids through our proximity, our influence, our words, and how we orient our lives in Christ.

As a parent, have you learned that values are more caught than taught?

Kids observe—and often absorb—them along the way.

Our kids bear witness to how we spend our money and our weekends.

Dinnertime and bedtime conversations shape them.

Our kids learn reconciliation not through taking Communion or giving insincere apologies to their siblings but by seeing us—their parents—make amends, tell on ourselves, and ask forgiveness. They have front-row seats to the message of God that we can illustrate. Home is God's laboratory for experimenting with hospitality by making room for Him. We all live, think, and act in accordance with whatever identity we adopt. And faith and family shape identity the most because identity is a narrative, not an accomplishment.

What makes the gospel good news is not just that it gives us something eternal to believe in.

It's good because it gives us a new *way to be* in the world.

We're part of a larger story! To restore creation, God launched a covenant family through Abraham (Genesis 15; Romans 4). He sent His Son into the world and sends His Spirit to help us even now.

If your kids haven't started asking why the world is the way it is, just wait until about third grade. When they do, rather than dismiss their difficult-to-answer questions, take them in stride. Host the conversations as often as your kids ask. When our kids were at this stage, I found it helpful to distinguish between the world we know as broken and impossible from the one God made and called good in these conversations. The Bible refers to the initial creation as "paradise."[8] So it's hard to imagine God intended the world to include things like COVID-19 and cancer; famine and natural disasters; miscarriages, divorce, and abuse. Ever since sin entered the human narrative, God's been working through covenant relationships to restore, redeem, and repair our stories.

> *As parents, hospitality means we embody Christ for our kids through our proximity, our influence, our words, and how we orient our lives in Christ.*

Being a child of God means we bear His image, which shapes our participation with God's mission in the world. Hospitality demonstrates the sending mission of God. He sent His Son, then His Spirit. Now He also sends His family. That doesn't mean every Christian travels the world as a missionary. To be Christian is to be sent, regardless of our day job or daily context. Wherever we go, we "host" God's presence, whether it be to our kids, our coworkers, our customers, our neighbors, or strangers. The image of God in you is intended to bear witness.

Understanding the missionary heart of God is central to reproducing Christian faith. The same God who sent His Son into the world sends us. In Acts 11:26, we read that Christ followers "were called Christians first at Antioch," not Jerusalem. Why Antioch? The disciples were sending people out! One of the most significant cultural shifts in the last generation is how many people relocate. With people constantly moving into our neighborhoods, schools, and offices, modern-day disciples can understand being sent to these familiar places as an assignment to receive, welcome, and care for a citywide network of neighbors. Christian hospitality reminds us of what it's like to be new, uninitiated, and disconnected while helping others feel like they belong.

Being a child of God means we bear His image, which shapes our participation with God's mission in the world.

GOSSIPING THE GOSPEL

Spiritual conversation in family life is a game-changing dynamic. Finding the words to describe our hope and why we follow Christ makes the biggest difference in our secular society. The challenge is finding the words to describe the difference Christ is making in our own lives. No one can argue with or refute your experience in Christ. For me, the most formative stories my parents shared always revolved around God's faithfulness to them. For example, Mom immigrated to the United States as an eleven-year-old, unable to speak English, who was trying to fit in while living in two cultures, and God saw her through that hard transition. And Dad grew up in a broken home but found new life in Christ at a

Billy Graham crusade, which changed the trajectory of his life—rooted in Christ, a loving husband of sixty-two years, a present dad with an endless desire to help and serve. Hearing my parents share experiences like these made a deep impact on my young self. The panoramas of their lives helped me view God as a faithful Friend because they shared the difference Christ was making in their lives with me.

In the early church, Christians faced stiff opposition from family and persecution from those in power. Faith was not something to be proclaimed loudly. Rather, early Christians had a peculiar lifestyle that might lead them to cautiously share their belief in the risen Christ with others. And yet the church grew like wildfire, mainly by their "gossiping of the gospel": The testimony of their lives led to intimate conversations. Early Christians "gossiped" the stories of how they fed the poor, tended to the sick, and adopted abandoned children. It's fascinating to me that despite worship being an invite-only, closed-to-the-public event, the early church grew from an estimated twenty-five thousand souls to twenty million in the first two hundred years![9]

Growing up, I was taught not to gossip, but sharing the Good News is something that positively can't be contained. Early Christians didn't make faith and community accessible through large-scale attractive events, media campaigns, or community programs. They assumed a posture of hospitality, making room for the most vulnerable while also hosting curious people who were witnesses to the almost contagious difference in them as they went about their everyday lives.

Spiritual conversation in family life is a game-changing dynamic.

Jesus' strategy for making disciples was never meant to mute the uniqueness of an individual's spiritual gifts. Reproduction isn't the same as replication. Then, as now, only so much of discipleship could be taught, but—because of the proximity, availability, and trustworthiness the disciples offered those drawn into their circles—the mission was "caught." New disciples went on to whisper the gospel in their own unique ways, and believers have been doing so ever since.

Cultivating a rhythm for hospitality invites us to talk about the difference God's story is making in our stories. Have you found the words to describe the difference Christ is making in you?

FINDING YOUR RHYTHM: EXPRESSING FAITH AS HOSPITALITY

Jesus sent out the seventy-two warning them they'd be like sheep among wolves *and* instructing them to take no provision with them (Luke 10:1-17). In going, they were to look for people of peace, those who showed kindness and general openness to them. Jesus said to proclaim the Kingdom of God to them (Luke 10:9), which I like to summarize as finding ways to talk about the difference Christ was making in them. Expressing faith as hospitality is about discerning whom God has prepared in advance for us. Whether you are on the giving or receiving end of hospitality, as a disciple you are to help others discover Christ through you.

People of peace are spiritual but not necessarily Christian. They might be new to your neighborhood, kids' schools, or workplace. They might have spiritual doubts, questions about God, or a history of church hurt, yet they show you favor and influence. What questions are they asking that you could help answer?

As you begin including them in your family prayers, try to hear their stories. Is there a need? What are their gifts? In what ways can you encourage, support, or receive from them? What kind of activity could you include them in (e.g., a family dinner or outing, a small group with other Christian families, a volunteer opportunity in your community)? If God has prepared you in advance with favor and influence, then God has also prepared you to reveal His care.

Make it your goal to identify three people of peace. List them below.

1.
2.
3.

An essential aspect of discipling our kids toward hospitality is describing the ongoing stories of our unfolding salvation experiences with God. Using these questions as prompts, consider your journey with Jesus. Think about key decisions, about moments of exhaustion, about God's faithfulness and your surrender to His lordship.

1. Try to find the words to describe how knowing Christ has shaped your desires, motivations, attitude, approach, and outlook. Respond in one to two sentences in the space below.

2. How has your definition of success changed since knowing Christ?

3. Where did you find your confidence, happiness, or security before becoming a Christian, and how are things different now? What changed?

4. How have your motivation, attitude, and desires changed since knowing Christ?

5. Are there any stories, illustrations, or metaphors that help describe your change of heart or how your relationship with Christ has grown?

6. What's something you really wanted, even prayed for, but never got . . . and it was for the best?

7. What causes have you discovered or concerns have you developed due to growing in Christ?

FINDING YOUR WINDOW:
MEALTIME, TRAVEL TIME, BEDTIME, AND MORNING TIME

Love the LORD your God with all your heart and with all your soul and with all your strength. These commandments that I give you today are to be on your hearts. Impress them on your children. Talk about them **when you sit** *at home and* **when you walk** *along the road,* **when you lie down** *and* **when you get up.**

DEUTERONOMY 6:5-7, *emphasis added*

"**When you sit**": At dinnertime, talk with your kids about what they want to do when they grow up. Try talking to them about who they want to be and what characteristics and qualities would help them succeed in God's eyes. What made Jesus successful? Ask how they might reflect God's love through their chosen occupations. If they dream of jobs that provide fame and wealth, ask them how God might use those skills and resources to help others thrive.

"**When you walk**": On your way to school, ask if there are any new kids who don't have anyone to sit with at lunch or play with at recess. Talk to your kids about how hard it is to be new or lonely. Challenge your kids to practice hospitality by inviting a new kid to sit or play with them. It's okay if the child doesn't turn out to be a best buddy; they'll still have had God's love displayed to them.

"**When you lie down**": At bedtime, ask your kids about which kids in their classes or on their teams have a hard time fitting in. Who gets teased often? If they can identify any kids acting mean or getting in trouble, ask them why they think that is. Remind your kids that those children are also created in God's image, and ask your kids how you can pray for them together.

"**When you get up**": In the morning, ask your kids how they think their teacher is doing. Is he or she tired, frustrated, or sad? See if you can find ways to coach your kids in empathy. Ask them to think of a way they can encourage their teacher, as if God wants them to be His messenger or instrument.

DIY DISCIPLEMAKING ACTIVITY #3

Back-to-School Blessing

THIS IS A UNIQUE CHANCE to practice hospitality as a family on the eve of a new school year. It can even be done with a faith family, your community, or neighbors. The idea is to have a fun activity, a short time of prayer, and a frozen treat to cap it off! Here are a few suggestions to help it work.

- Throw a straightforward one-hour front-yard party.

- Offer a variety of activities for different ages (sidewalk chalk, four square, bubbles, Spikeball, Twister, basketball, etc.).

- Use a backpack to give a five-minute object lesson. Talk about the baggage we can carry that weighs us down (taking tests; being embarrassed; losing friends; dealing with gossip, bad grades, mean kids, unfair teachers, etc.). These things happen to everyone at some point. The point is that we are not alone when we deal with hard things. Share a simple Scripture verse about God's promises to us, the hope we have in Christ, or how God gives us courage. Share a funny or embarrassing personal story, including how you survived or recovered. Or share about a great friendship you formed from an unlikely source that was part of God's care for you.

✿ Pray a blessing on kids (wisdom, protection, guidance; the new kid who just moved in with no one to sit with at lunch or a kid with special needs), parents (courage, faith, comfort), and teachers (strength, discernment, favor).

✿ Finish with a frozen treat.

CHAPTER 4

A RHYTHM IN COMMUNITY

Creating a Home Where We Make One Another Better

It's been said that we don't get to choose our families, which is a good reminder that they don't get to choose us either! One lady from the Deep South once spelled it out for my wife and me: "Honey, we're not asking if any of your family's crazy; we're wonderin' which ones." Then, after a laugh and a pause, she said, "And if nobody is comin' to mind, it might be you!"

Ever notice how family often becomes like the proverbial cat we kick at the end of a long day? In this scenario, the innocent pet gets hurt as an outlet for someone's bad mood. Now, I'm not suggesting that we physically kick our spouses or children (or cats, for that matter), but it's common to not reflect the love and affection we feel, especially after a long day or stressful meeting at work when there's a mound of dirty laundry and dinner isn't made yet. In public, we manage our appearances as best we can for as long as we can, but at some point (often when we get home), whatever's on the inside comes out. Most parents power through their days with relatively courteous exchanges with strangers and acquaintances, whatever they're feeling. And while the people around us might appreciate that we don't take out our feelings on them, our kids sure don't want to be our emotional scapegoats either. The problem is that as a society we don't know how to deal with our pain, stress, and disappointment. And those emotions don't go away without our naming, owning, and managing them.

So we store our feelings . . . for a while anyway.

For me, this reality became unsettling when I realized that sometimes people with whom I have casual interactions might get a way more pleasant version of me than those I care most about.

Think about the impressions we leave throughout the day with customers, coworkers, neighbors, waitstaff, grocery clerks, bank tellers, and parents in the school hallways. Most are positive, right? But once the garage door closes, the mask comes off. We let down our guard. And home can become *un*cherished ground.

This behavior makes sense. The people we feel closest to—the ones we know will always be around and the ones we have the longest history with—end up being the ones we make the slightest effort for. Instead of trying hard to guard our tongues, we let our guard down. Instead of showing patience, we come unglued. And it's all *because* we feel safe.

Safe that these people will always be family.

Safe that they won't reject us.

But when we feel safe without also restraining our tongues and tempers, we contaminate the otherwise fertile soil of family life.

Early on in parenthood, my wife and I coined a family motto: "Save your best for family." Rather than give our family the leftovers from any given day, we tried to intentionally offer our kids our best selves and encouraged them to do the same with us. Our appeal was "We get to enjoy what we create." I explained to our kids that, unlike their friends, who may come and go over the years, our family will always be in their lives. So it's worth the emotional effort. Their friends down the street or in the schoolyard shouldn't get a nicer or more patient version of them. When we experience each other's best selves at home, everyone benefits because we operate from a foundation of security, not performance or popularity.

I vividly remember one unsettling evening when I'd left the office but hadn't left the weight of it behind. Within the first ten minutes of being home, with dinner almost ready, I asked Bjørn to do something. I interrupted him from what he was doing to have him do what I wanted him to do. Distracted, he delayed. I'm not a yeller, but I snapped at him for not doing what I'd asked. After my impatient outburst, I felt worse than I had when I'd perceived him as ignoring me. Bjørn's always been a respectful kid and a good listener; this reaction revealed more about me than about him. So later that evening, I sat with him. "Bjørn, my reaction to you earlier wasn't right. I had a hard day, and I brought it home with me. I need to ask you to forgive me because I didn't save my best for our family. I took my stress out on you, and that wasn't right."

"Dad, it's okay. I didn't listen the first time."

"No, buddy. You're gracious, which I appreciate. But I don't want you to let me off that easily. I want to apologize because you shouldn't have to absorb my mistakes. I feel bad for making you feel bad."

"Dad," he replied, "I forgive you."

We've all been on the receiving end of an insincere apology, which doesn't accomplish anything. In order for him to truly forgive me, I wanted Bjørn to first acknowledge his disappointment.

That's what forgiveness is and does.

Conceding that we messed up frees our hearts from hurt and grudges.

It's hard to admit our flaws, but in discipling our kids with such honesty and humility, we demonstrate what reconciliation requires.

Families are safe when we cherish each member instead of taking our fears or stress out on them. We feel safe when we don't have to act like we're people we're not, strive for relentless goal setting, or make unhealthy comparisons.

But safety also requires loving restraint.

A home environment of safety doesn't mean we get to act however we want around our families knowing that they will still accept us. Safety invites us to come clean and own our mistakes. Kids see strength when we admit our impatience and overreactions. The safety of relationships requires us not to take those closest to us for granted. Saving our best for family was how my wife and I tried to instill a sense of belonging in our kids. Belonging isn't to be confused with being possessive or having ownership. Instead, it's the relational bond we share as parents, siblings, and family.

As believers, we also belong to God. *I am His, and He is mine. And even when I don't save my best for Him, I still belong.*

Our kids need to understand that we all belong to each other. Their choices affect Mom and Dad as much as our choices affect them. Their struggles are our struggles. Their wins are our wins. And just like with the way we belong to God, the nature of our relationship won't change. Practicing this kind of community as a family allows us to experience the ways God is raising us as we raise our kids.

THE GIFT (AND CHALLENGE) OF BEING CONSISTENT

Who doesn't like things to be easy? Life requires so much effort that it's hard not to be enticed by the idea that, somehow, the center of God's will is the path of least resistance.

But what if the path of least resistance is not often the center of God's will?

If the "blessed easier" were true, Jesus could've had His prayer answered and avoided the Cross. Parenting is more about helping our kids know Christ than about raising happy kids who are well liked.

One of the hardest parts of parenting is being consistent. All of us feel strongly about certain values. We prioritize certain behaviors. We have a picture of who we want our kids to become. *But* . . . after a long day or a late night, or when we're feeling rushed or distracted, it can be difficult to enforce the expectations we have of our kids.

Consistency might be a big challenge, but it's also one of the greatest gifts.

Kids are natural pleasers seeking their parents' approval. Even adults flourish when we know people and environments are predictable and social contracts are understood, present, and affirming. I suspect kids respond better to boundaries than rules.

In a family community, rules are typically assigned to the kids.

But boundaries apply to everyone.

The difference is that rules require obedience.

Boundaries create safety.

A fence is a helpful metaphor for a boundary. It serves as a physical boundary but has psychological effects too. A team of landscape architects conducted a simple but fascinating study to observe the impacts of having a fence around a playground. They first took preschoolers and their teacher to a playground with no fenced perimeter during their usual recess. The same group of kids was also taken to a comparable playground with a visible fenced boundary. Researchers found a striking difference in how the preschoolers interacted in each space. At the fenceless playground, the children "remained huddled around their teacher, fearful of leaving out of her sight." In the fenced playground, however, the kids maximized the entire playground, "feeling free to explore within the given boundaries."[1]

Boundaries are like weights parents lift to help families build emotional and spiritual strength. The "Save your best for family" motto was a boundary that helped my wife and I create a culture of what's expected and how each family member belongs. A dilemma parents face is that rules can seem much easier to define and enforce than boundaries. We feel subtly gratified once we deliver the rules, as if we're guiding and protecting our kids well. But rules never change lives. You could build a strong case that the greater our awareness of rules (particularly ones that apply to everyone), the more likely we are to revise the rules to fit our lives. This also explains why the government has little success when trying to legislate areas pertaining to morality. Having more rules doesn't make us better citizens any more than it makes us more Christlike.

AN OPEN-DOOR POLICY

Another boundary my wife and I tried to maintain in our home was an open-door policy. I'm not referring to being approachable to our kids, though we tried to cultivate that, too. Our open-door policy was literally about keeping doors open in the house. It was never a rule though. Doors were closed if a present was being wrapped or someone was studying and needed to concentrate or needed a little time and space to decompress. But when we went to bed at night, we kept the doors open. When someone was using the bathroom, doors were closed but typically unlocked. When everyone was getting ready for the day, it was never inappropriate for someone to come in while someone else was showering. The shower curtain provided privacy. Bjørn and Annika always shared the same bathroom and learned to be respectful, but the door was unlocked when one was in the shower and the other needed to brush their teeth to be on time for early-morning practice.

Discipling our kids meant encouraging them to walk in the light—figuratively and spiritually. By keeping doors unlocked and mostly open, my wife and I tried to make a statement to our kids that we had nothing to hide. It was a way of instilling a sense of character and integrity in them. I know this boundary isn't for everyone, but I share it to illustrate one way we tried to build a safe culture in our home. Remember, our homes are like laboratories to experiment with what we believe is true about God.

Open doors were also a way to illustrate the reality of God's presence.

He's with us in the hard and the good, when we're in the public eye and in our solitude!

Understanding that truth—and being comforted by it—requires practice. Living two lives (one based on reality and the other on lies) is a lot more work than living one. This was one small way we tried to disciple our kids with a culture of transparency and safety. Again, we sought to create fertile soil so the whole family could flourish. Many people grow up thinking God is angry and to be feared, and when I encounter this, I wonder how much of that perspective has been fueled by how the individual's family of origin handled boundaries. Too often we reenact what happened in the Fall. Privacy can lead to secrecy, and secrecy gave way to shame, fear, and regret in the Garden. As a result, Eve and Adam hid, covered up, and pointed the finger of blame. Small things, like a bite, make a big difference.

FEELINGS = WORDS

If you've ever watched *Mister Rogers' Neighborhood*, you've discovered a revolutionary wrapped in a cardigan on low-budget public television. He was a champion for the care of children—not by imposing rules on them but by creating healthy boundaries for them to express concern. We can't let Mister Rogers's gentle approach trick us into believing he wasn't a man of incredible conviction and strength. You can watch a YouTube video of him testifying on the Senate floor in 1969, explaining, "If we . . . can only make it clear that feelings are mentionable and manageable, we will have done a great service for mental health."[2] Talk about a modern-day prophet! Fred Rogers understood how to build a community (or neighborhood) because he understood boundaries.

There are two sounds that every parent can recognize. It's the difference between a genuine cry for help (because of injury or fear) and the sound of a child not getting their way. Tears and whining are unmistakable when they're about gaining attention, being exhausted, or getting what a child wants. My wife and I didn't always know how to help amid sniffles and tears and needed our kids to tell us what was wrong. Instead of being frustrated with a situation, we developed a phrase—"Use your words"—to help our kids explain how they felt. This served us well through their teen years. Our kids became more verbal, especially during challenging times. Perhaps the greatest value was the practice of putting words to how they felt about faith and communicating in relationships that meant the most.

Parents can impose their will when children are young. We take them where we are going, put them to bed on our schedule, and dole out permission and consequences as we see fit. But a shift occurs as kids enter adolescence. As their independence grows and influences beyond the home emerge, the way parents lead must evolve. We can no longer pick up our kids midtantrum, exit a store, and strap them in their car seats. Just as we want our children's verbal expression to develop, parents must find new ways to communicate and to navigate their kids' development.

Instead of leading by being authoritative, getting loud, or giving ultimatums, my wife and I had to lead our kids by influence.

Our discipline changed, as did our expectations.

We spoke of trust and expectations more than we threatened consequences.

We expressed concern and care but also experimented with incremental trust.

When it came to how we spoke to one another at home, we had words that were out of bounds. But the point of creating a communication culture wasn't to list the unacceptable words. Instead, it was about suggesting better ways to express our feelings.

Sometimes words seem to escape us like hot air escaping from a balloon.

When our kids were learning to talk, it was normal for them to blurt out what they wanted. Inevitably, it came out in the most primal and demanding ways, like "I wanna drink!" Instead of correcting them or setting rules about being respectful—or dismissing their tone because they were young—we tried to create a boundary by responding, "Oh, I'd love to get you something to drink, but is there another way you can say that?" Without fail, they'd reframe their demand as a polite question. Creating a community at home—where Christ can be known—is directly tied to how we use our words. This was one way we all got to enjoy the respectful atmosphere we created.

When we think of God's commands, it's easy to view them as rules restricting us from pleasure or freedom. But God's commands were designed to help us live in harmony with Him, each other, and creation. They are healthy boundaries outlining a path for us to flourish. A rule would say, "You're not allowed to hit your sister." Did we have rules about not hitting? Sure. To this day, our two kids, with different personalities, have never struck each other. They've fussed at, argued with, and gotten mad at each other, as siblings do. But I tried to frame our expectations with a picture of what home can look like by asking, "Do you like it when you feel trusted? Do you want an enemy at home or a friend?"

Friendship requires respect, but this question was a way to offer our kids agency to pursue a quality relationship like the one we can enjoy with God. Parents who desire to instill hearts for God and animate faith create room for grace and truth. I'm not opposed to rules—some rules are necessary for keeping kids safe ("Let's hold hands in the parking lot," "Don't accept rides or gifts from strangers," "Be true to your word," and "Wear clean underwear daily," for example). We had them too. But rather than being strict with our kids, Laurel and I worked at being consistent with them. Instead of a chain of command, we experimented with a chain of care.

CONTRIBUTIONS GROW COMMUNITY

I recall one Friday evening when Annika was fifteen and a half years old, having just obtained her learner's permit. I suggested we go out to eat, and she immediately asked, "Can I drive?" Suddenly, Tex-Mex didn't sound as good. "Sure, Annika," I said shakily with a fake smile.

The parking lot of Matt's El Rancho is always crowded and has skinny parking spots. As we made our way through congested aisles, a hurried driver in a large truck was trying to exit. He was revving his engine and lurching forward in a four-car congested choke point. My nervous daughter was waiting for things to clear without room to get out of anyone's way. From the passenger seat, I signaled for him to wait. But this impatient rancher decided to force his way through instead. Turning left with wheels as high as our window, he approached the driver's side, rubbed his huge tires along the front quarter panel, and forced his way past us.

And he just kept going.

Without thinking (maybe because I felt threatened, or maybe because I've watched too many Jason Bourne action movies), I unbuckled my seat belt, unlocked the car door, and began sprinting across the parking lot in hot pursuit.

Being fleet of foot is not the same as being drunk on adrenaline and *thinking* fast on your feet.

As this monster truck starter kit reached the driveway to exit, I caught up. With two hands, I grabbed his tailgate, which is when it occurred to me: *What's my plan?*

In Texas, a man in an oversize truck in a hurry bullying his way through a parking lot has a *high* probability of having firearms with him.

I hadn't thought about having a rational conversation, since this wasn't a clear-eyed moment for me. So I did what anyone does when confronting a grizzly bear, mountain lion, or kitchen mouse . . . I yelled. Not in a deep or imposing way; I was more like a spoiled kid whining that his sister isn't sharing.

"Hey, you just hit us!!!"

Acting unaware of the obvious, he rolled down his window and said, "Oh . . . I did?"

This man—with eyelids at half-mast, having just left happy hour—climbed out of the truck barefoot to slur his way to responsibility.

Parenting eager would-be drivers can test the seaworthiness of any family ship floating in community. But this teenage ritual can also deepen the relationship when they see you as for them.

There are tears (her),

raised voices (us),

stern directions (me),
real fear (me),
false confidence (her),
a profound need for approval (her),
and a good bit of forced affirmation (me).

This gauntlet of teenage independence also represents a coming-of-age for parents. And, like a second tour of duty, it doesn't get easier with the next child. You want your kids to be successful. You want to trust them. And you know these growing pains are normal and good.

Parenting is a unique way to "grow up in [our] salvation" (1 Peter 2:2). Just as salvation is based on a growing relationship with God while navigating varied circumstances, parenting at each stage is making sense of all life's challenges. Sometimes we follow Christ with reckless abandon and passion. Other times we follow obediently or even out of obligation. It's hard to feel prepared, confident, or poised; too often, that paralyzes earnest followers of Jesus from investing.

But this is what disciplemaking is: instilling what we do have while depending on the Spirit to provide for what we need.

COMING OF AGE

Coming of age *in Christ* and understanding our spiritual adoption have a life-changing effect on our perspective. Once we put our faith in Christ, we are adopted as God's sons and daughters. Paul wrote to a group of new Christians in Galatia about coming of age spiritually (Galatians 4:1-7). We tend to think being a child of God means we're helpless and only able to receive from Him. Adoption in Scripture, however, means accepting the privileges and responsibilities of a full-grown heir. In other words, God saves us with the idea that we will mature into trusted contributors to the Kingdom of Heaven on earth.

In ancient Rome, it was more common for people to adopt adults than babies, who could be considered burdensome. In a culture without Medicare or retirement savings, aging couples without heirs would "legally adopt a young man whom they loved and trusted to take over the family business . . . so the couple would be taken care of in their old age."[3]

Similarly, God has placed us in a spiritual family and wants us to live with a new identity.

We are invited to come of age as trusted heirs!

Our heavenly Father adopts us, but not as helpless children. Instead, we're invited to be valued contributors to our Father's business.

As much as my wife and I sought to set our kids up to win, to create soil for them to grow in Christ, we understood that we couldn't parent alone. We needed the church to be our community—an extended family of faith. We continually gave, served, supported, and celebrated with other families in our church community, *and* we also received God's care via spiritual brothers and sisters, aunts and uncles, and grandparents. We saw the need—and God's provision—in people who had been married longer than us, in people who had parented longer or walked further in their journeys, having had more experiences in terms of careers, relocations, injuries, health scares, and faith lives.

Historically, the people of God held faith as a collective. In ancient Israel, children were discipled within an extended family of faith. As generations married and built their homes onto existing ones, they'd often created a housing complex called an insula—a cluster of multilevel buildings where extended families lived around a central courtyard. The insula (think: "*insula*tion") was a compound-like structure with additional rooms for grown-up children beginning their own nuclear families.[4] It was where generations came to understand that one's problems, parents, or resources weren't theirs alone. In an insula, there was collective wisdom and the safety of being known without the fear of rejection. When a marriage struggled, someone who had been married longer would be on hand to help by sharing from their own experience. Other influential adults could reinforce an important message when parents felt they were losing their influence over their kids.

Like marriage and family, faith is always a team sport. We discover this truth when a local faith community, or church, becomes an extended family of faith. Members play to one another's strengths, help one another through struggles, and speak to one another's personal potential (and even blind spots!) because they've developed trusted rapport together. For disciplemaking parents, this essential group often reveals subtle ways God is raising us while we are raising our kids.

Parents don't need to be right to be righteous.

Our children are more likely to see Christ in us as we admit fault, take responsibility, and receive the grace that awaits us than when we attempt to hide our weaknesses and imperfections.

They also see the friends we draw near, receive from, and sacrifice for, followers of Christ whose lives display the same message of God's eternal hope we strive to share with our kids. Arguably, our greatest reward in life is when we advocate for another person's success. Parenting brings both immeasurable joy and profound heartache because we are so deeply invested in our kids' success. Homegrowing disciples is transformational because it requires us, like Jesus, to give ourselves to see our families and communities flourish. God is loving us as we love others. He's raising us while we raise our kids. I suspect that, by His grace, God is closer to your family than you might imagine, and He will use your faith community to help you and your kids sense His presence palpably in your day-to-day lives . . . as both givers *and* receivers.

FINDING YOUR RHYTHM: YOUR DEVELOPMENTAL COMMUNITY

Since faith and family are always better as team sports, take a 360-degree inventory of the developmental influences in your life. This exercise is designed to help you see a tangible expression of God's community. With some people you list, you'll be more on the receiving end of the spectrum, while with others you'll be more on the giving end. But everyone you identify is someone through whom God reveals Himself and your need for Him. We grow God's Kingdom on earth together.

The 360-degree inventory typically works best if you work on your list two or three times over a couple of days. You might also try praying the first few verses of Psalm 139 alongside it. Read slowly, waiting for the Spirit to bring names or faces to mind. As you identify people who have influenced you, you may find it helpful to consider the following four categories:

1. **Mentors** are simply people who are further along in a certain aspect of life who intentionally share wisdom with you, make themselves available to you, and are invested in your well-being. Identify three mentors below. Alongside each name, name which category they influence (faith, marriage, career, parenting, etc.).

2. People in **your inner circle** are those closest to you who share your faith, can sense when something is amiss, can speak to your strengths, and have your best interests at heart. (Think of the ones who are the healthiest emotionally and spiritually, ideally those who live locally and with whom you're able to be accountable.)

3. **Your tribe** consists of your extended faith family. They also might be from different life stages, backgrounds, or cultures. These are people whom you respect and who have observed you and know your family and likely share your faith.

4. **Foes** are people you are at odds with who are still part of your life. These are the people you tend to avoid being around. For each person you identify, it might also be helpful to name the offense that's created a rift.

FINDING YOUR WINDOW:
MEALTIME, TRAVEL TIME, BEDTIME, AND MORNING TIME

Love the LORD your God with all your heart and with all your soul and with all your strength. These commandments that I give you today are to be on your hearts. Impress them on your children. Talk about them **when you sit** *at home and* **when you walk** *along the road,* **when you lie down** *and* **when you get up.**

DEUTERONOMY 6:5-7, *emphasis added*

"When you sit": At dinnertime, go around the table two or three times, focusing on one person at a time. Have each person describe how that individual makes you better.

"When you walk": On your way to school, ask, "Do you think a person can communicate without using words?" Certainly we can, but the point is to get initial buy-in for the conversation. Continue, "What's an example of a kind or positive way we can communicate using just our eyes? What's a negative or hurtful way to use just our eyes?" Try this question using our ears and hearing, then hands and touch. The goal is to help your kids be more aware of how they can reflect the kindness of Jesus and care for others, even if they don't have the words to say. Follow up with them after school to see if they noticed any wordless communication (that was kind or not).

"When you lie down": At bedtime, discuss the idea of how you could "save your best for family." It's not just about being nicer to one another; we want to care for one another as if Jesus is present. We want family members to feel as safe and accepted with us as we do with God. Try following up this suggestion by confessing a recent situation that you could've handled better, like an impatient moment when you spoke harsh words. Begin with "Yesterday, I didn't save my best for family when I . . ." End with "Will you forgive me?" See if anyone else wants to offer their own confession.

"When you get up": In the morning, play with the metaphor of how being in a relationship can mirror being on a car ride. Some drives are long while others are short. Sometimes we get stuck in traffic and it stresses us out, while other times our car rides are at high speed on the open road. Some trips are to familiar places; others involve us getting lost along the way. Some car rides are bumpy or smooth, paved, muddy, slippery. See what parallels your kids offer as they use this metaphor to evaluate their own relationships: What does time at recess or lunch, in the locker room, or with their soccer team feel like? Ask your child to describe their closest friends, their siblings, your family, and/or their relationship with Jesus in terms of a car ride and discuss their insights.

DIY DISCIPLEMAKING ACTIVITY #4

Growing in Community

DISCUSS THE FOLLOWING community-building ideas with your family, and come up with a plan to implement them. Over the next month, try to practice one individually, another as a family, and the third with a small group.

- Ask about the bigger story of someone else's life (perhaps starting with a pivotal moment or a hidden talent, accomplishment, or hobby and when it began), particularly someone from another life stage, background, and/or experience. This person may have been a mere acquaintance beforehand, but hearing their deeper story will give you greater insight into who they are. Maybe a friendship will develop!

- Make an actionable plan to start celebrating key markers in people's lives—birthdays, anniversaries, promotions, housewarmings, the birth of children. Start with the people you are closest to in your faith community. Don't wait for social media to remind you. Keep your own records.

- Find a parent in your faith community, at your kids' schools, or from their extracurriculars who needs help (e.g., a recent divorcée, a single parent, or someone who just relocated). How can you and your family or community be part of the response to a prayer for comfort, encouragement, or blessing? Come up with ways you can offer help in the next month.

CHAPTER 5

A RHYTHM OF COMPASSION

Seeing Others' Needs as Different from Our Own

I TAKE A WINDOW SEAT for a three-hour flight, and a couple in their fifties joins my row. The man sits in the middle seat, sending all the wrong signs. He's bothered. They're not talking much, but he strikes me as rude. Maybe they just had a disagreement. As we take off, he leans past the armrest to peer out the window over my shoulder with the curiosity of a little kid. I pull out my laptop and lean away. When he looks away, I pull my shade. He begins scrolling through videos on his phone without earbuds, and the volume is cranked up. I shake my head, thinking, *This is gonna be a long flight.* Then he places his drink order—two whiskeys with Coke. *Ugh, I hope he doesn't get belligerent.* After the first beverage service, he orders another round. I think, *Someone needs to cut him off. This guy needs an intervention.* Shortly after his second round, we begin our descent. I open my shade to see our destination.

Immediately, the man snaps his neck to look, once again leaning in. I think, *What's his problem?*

I see the man and his wife whispering, leaning toward each other, as she reaches to hold his hand.

Then it dawns on me in my self-righteous, compassion-lacking state: *This guy isn't an alcoholic fueling his addiction. This guy's battling a real fear!*

Fear of heights? Flying? Enclosed spaces?

Is he on his way to bury a loved one? Be reunited with his birth father?

The man is desperately trying to cope without making a scene. He is facing his fears while I'm bothered, unaware of what he's going through. I can't imagine this trip was his first choice.

I confessed this experience to my family over dinner that night. I wanted to own my fault in hopes that I will react differently next time. It was a teaching moment for all of us. I hoped my kids could learn from, maybe be inspired by, the Spirit convicting me. They've seen my weak moments, but they also know I mean well and how easy it is for all of us to judge someone in any given moment.

Being compassionate involves discovering how God is loving us and our kids even as we learn to love others. It helps us to confess that while others' needs might be different from our own, we're all in need of grace.

What I'm still learning is that compassion requires an inspired strength in the same way confession does. Both are rooted in a desire to embody God's love. Confession is always safe when love and acceptance are present. Compassion bears witness to God's gracious care for us and our families. Being compassionate involves discovering how God is loving us and our kids even as we learn to love others. It helps us to confess that while others' needs might be different from our own, we're all in need of grace.

FAITH IN THE WILD

It's one thing to witness a snake in an aquarium-like setting behind glass. It's a completely different, adrenaline-fueled encounter when one greets you in your tent.

It's one thing to watch a game from your couch, where you have convenient access to bathrooms, food, drink, and the thermostat. But it can feel like the world is orbiting that same game when you're immersed in a sold-out stadium and are emotionally invested in every play.

It's one thing to listen to a soundtrack of your favorite musical. It's another thing to see the pageantry live, close enough to get lost in the plot and be moved by the singers' facial expressions and vocal ranges.

Nothing captures us like being in a native context.

The freedom of religion we enjoy here in the West can make faith seem like something to be observed on Sundays more than lived all week long.

We opt for the safe confines of church over the incarnational adventure of encountering God in the world.

And yet God is at work in the world as much as He brings revelation in church.

The difference between the two contexts is as different as a lecture is from a laboratory, singing in the shower versus performing on a stage, playing a video game at your leisure or experiencing the thrill of winning on a field when the game is on the line.

A rhythm of compassion helps us and the kids in our care experience God's revelation "in the wild." It moves faith from a familiar environment of consuming knowledge about God to a moving encounter with God's righteousness, redemption, and restoration.

We celebrate Immanuel, God with us, and *compassion* means "to suffer with."¹ Just as Jesus was sent, the concept of compassion suggests we are sent to stand in solidarity with others. The basis for God's intervention is because He is compassionate and gracious (Exodus 34:6). "I've seen the suffering, the misery of my people . . . heard their cry," the Lord exclaims in Exodus (Exodus 3:7, author's paraphrase). Think about it this way: As parents, we can't stand idly by as our kids suffer and struggle. In the same way, God suffers in our woundedness, loss, selfishness, and pride. God seeks to enter our humanity with compassion and grace. God's heart breaks for those who are vulnerable and in need of grace.

In coming of age as disciples—at every age—we have much to gain in being intentional about crossing social, economic, and cultural divides.

Rather than expecting us to simply raise our kids within the familiar confines of a church, God gave us His Son and the Spirit to incarnate faith in the world. We can reproduce the hope we have in our children by following Christ's example and the Spirit's guidance. In coming of age as disciples—at every age—we have much to gain in being intentional about crossing social, economic, and cultural divides.

If my faith paradigm creates a life that avoids sacrifice and discomfort and standing with those who suffer, I'm not fully living in God's story. God invites His children to stand in solidarity with others as part of the salvation He offers humans. Parenting can illustrate how little control we have. Try as we might, plan as we do, we can't insulate our kids with Bubble Wrap to insulate them from personal hardship or the brokenness around them. However, discipling them in the way of Jesus and responding with compassion to others shapes a living hope in them. What we know already—and what our kids desperately need to learn—is that God dwells in both the hard and the good! The best thing we can do for our children is make the voice of the Good Shepherd familiar to them so they will follow His lead.

Compassion is God's love infused with His Spirit, wrapped in human flesh, then sent to put the divine on display.

COMPASSIONATE PLAYDATES

One of the fun ways my community has sought to live on mission as families is by finding friendships at an emergency foster-shelter facility. This place houses kids ranging from six to seventeen years of age who have been orphaned. Our small faith community has embraced the motto "We throw parties for the sake of others." For example, we once hosted these kids at a dock on Lake Austin. None of them had been on a ski boat before, which surprised some of our own kids. And none of them had been on a one-hundred-foot-long Slip 'N Slide. We won't solve the problems associated with broken home lives by throwing parties, but when smiles and belly laughs emerge with enthusiastic teenage thank-yous, if only for a day, it feels like heaven crashing into earth.

On another occasion, our faith community rented an outdoor laser tag game for some of these kids. Before the van arrived with our guests, I explained the complicated nature of their family situations to our families. I challenged our families to be the hosts, initiate conversations, and work to make these dozen kids feel welcome. And I offered this challenge: Today, everyone needs to learn someone's name, use it so the person hears it, and then pray for them this week as a family. Intermixing teams of six- to seventeen-year-olds from both groups helped us meet on a level playing field. Afterward, we enjoyed water bottles and Popsicles. We broke into family groups for simple but fun conversations with appropriate guided questions to avoid prying into our guests' stories or trauma.

We have only to look to discover vulnerable people whom God has placed in our path. Compassion is always an exercise of recentering, beckoning us away from orbiting our comfort levels. Service projects are a good place to start, but the real impact happens when a relationship grows. We dignify each other by giving and receiving in our own unique ways. And once we find people to learn from, we begin figuring out how to receive from them. Compassion is learning to see others' needs as simply different from our own. In the end, we're all in need in one way or another. Beautiful things can happen when we operate from this reality, opening ourselves to the Holy Spirit's guidance.

WHO IS MY NEIGHBOR?

In Jeremiah 29, we find Israel conquered despite being God's chosen people. While they prayed for deliverance, God responded, saying, "Seek the peace and prosperity of the city to which I have carried you into exile. Pray to the LORD for it, because if it prospers, you too will prosper" (Jeremiah 29:7). This command was for the whole city.

What if Jesus' command to love our neighbor (Matthew 22:39) requires more of us than simply being kind to those living on our block?

What if we're invited to care for people whose needs differ from ours as part of our disciplemaking impact?

Typically, neighbors living in proximity have similar incomes, education levels, and opportunities to ours. Yet Jesus' nudge to love our neighbor suggests those who are *unlike* us.

Whose suffering have you seen? Whose hardships have your

children asked you about? A prompt to show compassion might seem like an interruption to your day. It'll likely feel uncomfortable. It might cost you something. Standing in solidarity with people whose needs differ from our own requires us to climb up on the lap of the one who gives good gifts (Matthew 7:11). When we miss these opportunities, it's like we've walked through the mall at Christmastime without noticing Santa—and our kids miss out too.

Discipling our families with a rhythm of compassion is a sacred part of God's revelation in the world. Compassion reveals God's missionary heart. He sent His Son to earth . . . and He, in turn, sends us out into the world.

The practice of personal and family rhythms of compassion often leads us to unlikely sources of encouragement. Along with our faith community, my family spent a lot of time visiting apartment complexes that housed new arrivals from Afghanistan. One time we were sitting on the floor in a bare apartment drinking chai and eating hummus, dates, and almonds with our newfound friends. I asked their seventh-grade daughter if she had made any American friends yet. She said no. Pressing further, I asked if the American kids were curious about her story. With tears in her eyes, she pointed to her hijab and said, "They ask me why I have to wear this." It was such a tender moment: The preteen was navigating two cultures at once in an already awkward life stage, and like her American peers, she simply wanted to fit in.

Compassion reveals God's missionary heart. He sent His Son to earth . . . and He, in turn, sends us out into the world.

Witnessing her struggle was a humanizing experience for me. I couldn't help but see my own adolescent kids in my young friend, and I empathized with her. And I saw the Father's love for her. In his book *Loving Samaritans*, pastor Terry Crist writes, "As we trace Jesus' steps from Jerusalem to Samaria, a question arises: What would it mean to follow in his footsteps, to see beyond 'us' and 'them,' and to embrace every person on our journey with love and understanding?"[2] As followers of Christ, it's a holy adventure to seek to find out. When the roots of compassion deepen, faith and relationships grow. These friendships reveal the fullness of God in humanity.

COMPASSION BREATHES NEW LIFE

Having a family rhythm of compassion helps our kids regularly experience what grace is like. The wonderful thing about God's grace to us is that we don't deserve it and don't do anything to earn it. When we extend grace to others, our gestures may not always be appreciated or even acknowledged—and that's okay. Since our kids start out living in the shadow of our faith, they apprentice us as we experience firsthand the Word being flesh (John 1:14).

In our faith community, we tried creating "labs" to experiment with this rhythm and complement the learning taking place in Sunday kids' groups. We organized weekly ESL classes and often hosted baby showers with Burmese families that included brunch and prayers. One of these showers was particularly memorable. As I made my way to the apartment of the expectant mother, Faith, my mood shifted.[3] Low-rent apartments frustrate me because the people living in them tend to be taken advantage of since they often can hardly speak the local language and aren't accustomed to the kind of self-advocacy Americans learn growing up in the States. Not surprisingly, almost everyone renting in this complex was foreign born. Myanmar has been under military rule more years than not since gaining its independence from Britain in the mid-1900s.[4] Understandably, it's common for Burmese people to avoid making eye contact. Imagine how the idea of making requests might seem to someone who grew up under military rule! Climbing three stories, I grew upset seeing how worn and uneven the wooden steps were, making them a tripping hazard. Spindles were missing from the railings, posing a safety risk for small children, who could fall through the gaps. At the top, I thought, *I wouldn't want to live here. This neglected complex is depressing. It feels like hell on earth.*

But then I entered the brunch party, and it was like stumbling through the wardrobe into Narnia—after the witch has been defeated.

Before me lay a fantastic spread of food and elegantly wrapped gifts from our community of children, singles, families, and empty nesters. After giving hugs all around, we all piled into the apartment and heard Faith's story. Fleeing Myanmar, she and her husband and five-year-old son had traveled on foot for three weeks through the Thailand jungle, hiding from soldiers since they had no money to bribe them not to give them away. After arriving in Malaysia, Faith lived in a ten-foot-by-ten-foot shelter for eight years, giving birth to two girls over that time frame. Her unemployed husband took to alcohol and ended up leaving her and the children. Eventually Faith was granted the chance to relocate by the United Nations, and she chose to move to Austin, Texas. God met her like in the parable of the persistent widow who keeps calling for justice and mercy.

As I listened to Faith speak, my "hell on earth" perspective shifted. Suddenly heaven felt very near.

While she shared her story, Faith kept praising God for being with her all along. With tears, she described the wealth of her faith and community here. She praised God for giving her children the opportunity for education, for putting a roof over their heads, and for giving them access to health care, clean water, and indoor plumbing. She thanked God for the health of her children, a Christian husband, and the birth of a new son.

God was speaking through Faith in that moment.

I saw only darkness and despair, but she saw light.
I saw unacceptable conditions. She saw provision.
I saw hell, but she described heaven on earth.
I saw a cave, but she discovered it was but a tunnel.

A rhythm of compassion becomes a gateway to resensitize our hearts as parents, spouses, and children of God. When you find yourself getting cynical or sense that your children do not recognize God's provision, try finding people whose material needs differ from your own. Trust that God can resurrect new life in your family as you care for others.

WHO IS MY HELPER?

So far in this chapter, I've mostly illustrated a rhythm of compassion as engaging in boundary-crossing encounters—which is important because Jesus confronted those who were not sensitive to the needs among them. This is why I've tried to provide some imagination, perhaps even inspiration, for how parents can illustrate how faith can be leveraged for others' benefit.

The need for compassion and a sensitive heart also exists at home. Patience, kindness, and sacrifice of personal preference are also hard to sustain when it comes to your own immediate family. It's not that our love for our children fades but that sometimes, amid our daily demands, we find ourselves responding to them with impatience, reactivity, or even unkindness. It's in these moments we best understand that God isn't sitting in heaven with a red pen grading us like we're unmotivated students. Instead, the Holy Spirit enters our humanity with a deposit of grace that is sufficient for us.

It's one thing to know that the Holy Spirit is real, but it's another thing to know how the Spirit works. This is why discipleship is not simply growing in knowledge, volunteering more, and learning more liturgy. Rather, our faith grows as we learn to notice and align ourselves with God's activity in the world.

The Holy Spirit is God's provision to help us live the lives we've been called to live but can't sustain on our own. God's Spirit moves us emotionally and gives us agency for compassion as well as things like forgiveness, grace, and generosity. From the moment we first believe, we experience the indwelling of God's Holy Spirit. Jesus has also promised His disciples another baptism. The infilling of the Holy Spirit is what we can't imagine, accomplish, or give strength to through human effort.

The following list is what my wife and I used to help our children understand the ministry of the Holy Spirit.[5] It's not exhaustive, but it's a helpful start for disciplemaking parents seeking to teach their children how to discern the Spirit's disciplemaking work in and through their lives. The Holy Spirit gives us . . .

A greater capacity to love. We all encounter people who are hard to love. Maybe they have different opinions from ours or have done things to hurt us. Love is a Christian's greatest salve to heal a struggling marriage, a prodigal child, a soured friendship, or difficult supervisor. The Holy Spirit can meet us in our weaknesses and human limitations and help us express compassion, care, grace, patience, and mercy. If you want to find evidence of the Holy Spirit, ask questions like *Do I love God more now than I did a year ago? Do I grieve injustice more? Do I find more beauty in creation and diversity? Am I more patient, and is my heart more sensitized to the Spirit's guidance?* Beyond rational sense, the Spirit helps us love even the most hard-to-love people.

A greater power for obedience. Compassionate obedience is difficult, if not impossible, to sustain when we depend on sheer willpower or charitable moods. Yet God calls each of us into obedience, not as a burden or obligation but out of love (1 John 5:3). God also knows our needs. The Holy Spirit is often evidence of God's presence empowering us to turn from temptation, help without being asked, give without being recognized, or obey even when our strength and courage are lacking.[6] Imagine discipling your kids into a Spirit-led understanding. From our own experience, we explain how, over time, we realize that activities, words, and thoughts that once seemed like no big deal now seem problematic. The Holy Spirit has a way of "courting" us by giving us a moment of pause or hesitation. Other times, the Spirit might compel us to turn toward or away from an idea, attitude, person, or behavior.

A greater boldness in our witness. Have you ever had a conversation with someone in a desperate place in which you shared meaningful insight, counsel, or comfort? You didn't prepare for it and couldn't re-create the conversation if you tried. What's more, it's difficult to recall precisely what you said. All you know is that you helped. Other times, perhaps you feel compelled to share personal experiences—a question gets asked, an observation is made, or an idea is shared, and before you talk yourself out of it, a conversation has begun, and the Spirit guides it. The compulsion to bear witness to Christ is often prompted by the work of the Spirit.[7] A significant part of the deepening work of God's Spirit is that we respond to our God-prompted convictions in increasing measure over time. Doing so can move us to advocacy, relief work, and sacrificial choices. It might even mean becoming part of the answer to our prayer requests.

A greater openness to forgiveness.[8] Immediately after telling the story of Jesus' resurrection, John's Gospel shares Jesus' teaching about how the Holy Spirit helps us do what we can't or don't want to do on our own: "Again Jesus said, 'Peace be with you! As the Father has sent me, I am sending you.' And with that he breathed on them and said, 'Receive the Holy Spirit. If you forgive anyone's sins, their sins are forgiven; if you do not forgive them, they are not forgiven'" (John 20:21-23). Another way we encounter the Holy Spirit's strength is through our capacity to give and receive forgiveness. It might not feel wanted or warranted, but learning to do this becomes the greatest Christian deposit we can make in our children's lives. When our kids were little, my wife and I encouraged them to move past simple apologies. We've all received an insincere apology like "Well, I'm sorry you took it that way" (. . . but you're not sorry you did it?). Asking for forgiveness invites consent. We can't control another's response, but it gives a person we've hurt the opportunity to release their offense. Compassion is a form of forgiveness—it always requires faith because it makes us vulnerable on some level. For our kids, asking for forgiveness was a way to own what was their fault and learn to unburden their hearts. Letting go of resentment when we've been wronged is one of the hardest things to do, but resentment robs us of confidence, joy, and intimacy. Our family wasn't perfect at forgiving each other, but our openness to this kind of vulnerability created a culture of acceptance, safety, and second chances.

Verbal expression. One of the initial demonstrations of the Holy Spirit in the early church was what came out of the believers' mouths. In the book of Acts, when the Holy Spirit came upon the disciples, they "spoke the word of God boldly" (Acts 4:31), spoke words of knowledge (see Acts 5:1-11), and spoke in tongues and prophesied (Acts 2:4; 19:6). Stephen's accusers "could not stand up against the wisdom the Spirit gave him as he spoke" (Acts 6:10), and Gentiles were "speaking in tongues and praising God" (Acts 10:46).

Verbal expression is consistently associated with the manifestation and ongoing activity of the Holy Spirit. If we learn anything from Pentecost, we learn that the Holy Spirit transcends tradition, culture, ethnicity, and religion: The Galilean disciples were "declaring the wonders of God in [foreign languages]" (Acts 2:11). Verbal expression is an essential part of the Christian incarnation, and our words are a significant way to reflect God's character and nature. In discipling our kids, it's worth explaining that our speech can bear just as much fruit as our deeds. It might take some reorienting, but try to imagine using speech to express faith in God and extend compassion to others. This is how the Holy Spirit is revealed in our conversations and worship. Conversely, curses, accusations, criticism, gossip, and innuendos only reveal what's in the heart. They're neither a helpful witness nor evidence that the Holy Spirit is active in one's heart.

The fruit of the Spirit. The Holy Spirit does more than help us modify our behaviors and act like nice Christians; the fruit of the Spirit reveals change from the inside out. The fruit described in Galatians 5:22-23—love, joy, peace, patience, kindness, goodness, faithfulness, gentleness, and self-control—is the by-product of a heart that's been realigned and oriented with God's heart. For instance, showing self-control and kindness to a client after a deal falls through and then coming home and taking out your frustration on your family is not evidence of the Spirit doing inner work in you. The Spirit doesn't keep us from experiencing loss, fear, or stress. But the Spirit sustains our faith and hope and encourages us to seek comfort in God's grace.

One helpful way to start explaining the Holy Spirit's role to your children is by using the metaphor from Scripture of Him as an advocate (John 14:16, 26; 15:26; 16:7). We can make many connections to advocates, from friends to lawyers to parents to Jesus. Simply put, *advocating* means acting on someone else's behalf. We can be a compassionate advocate for underserved people in our cities.

THE POWER OF GOOD WORKS

What happens when *Shark Tank* meets "Love your neighbor"? You get an exciting event called The Pitch. To celebrate the Kingdom of Heaven in Austin, our community of families cobbled together two thousand dollars. Together with our extended faith community, we invited three local, volunteer-led nonprofits to come and make a pitch to us. I said, "You have eight minutes to tell us your mission and history, explain how you are loving our Austin neighbors, and share what you'd do with one thousand dollars. We'll vote, and a simple majority wins one thousand dollars. The two runners-up get five hundred dollars each, and we all eat amazing brisket BBQ." Playing with our rhythms of compassion and generosity, we wanted to sow seeds in other small, bootstrapping organizations to encourage them. It was a fun way to include hopeful skeptics and encourage neighbors to invest in the Kingdom locally. At the night's end, an older lady approached me and shared, with a serious tone, "I am not a Christian, but I believe everything you said about God tonight." The funny thing is that all I talked about were rhythms of generosity and compassion.

Along with several other families, in discipling our kids, my wife and I tried to instill wonder, curate curiosity, and make faith and community accessible. For The Pitch, our invitation was simple: "Come be a 'shark' and help us give away money!" All three directors of the participating organizations were young moms, working day jobs and leading their nonprofits because opportunities had found them. Each did a wonderful job describing their mission. While collecting the votes, one lady said she couldn't decide, then smiled and said, "David, let's make sure they all win," which was code for making three one-thousand-dollar on-the-spot donations so that each organization received a one-thousand-dollar check at the end of the night.

Compassion helps us understand the kind of world that God intended and saves us from thinking we're each the center of our own story.

The Hebrew word *tsedaqah* can mean both "righteousness" and "charity." Righteousness isn't being perfect but being right with God. The apostle Paul said, "God made him who had no sin to be sin for us, *so that* in him we might become the righteousness of God" (2 Corinthians 5:21, emphasis added). We display a living Christ to a desperate, anxious world when hope and compassion course through our veins and pour out our lips.

Practicing compassion, generosity, and hospitality won't make us perfect, but it can make us righteous. If we're too busy with our kids' sports, dance, and music lessons to connect with vulnerable and marginalized people, we'll never meet them. Worse, our children won't see these rhythms as a central way God meets the world's needs. Compassion helps us understand the kind of world that God intended and saves us from thinking we're each the center of our own story.

FINDING YOUR RHYTHM: EMBRACING A NEW IDENTITY AS A NEW CREATION

Jesus' resurrection introduced both a new covenant and a new humanity. New Testament writers like Paul picked up on this new identity. Showing compassion as an act of service or to give someone another chance requires faith because it makes us vulnerable to another's response. Having our identity in Christ helps us become more comfortable in our own skin—first by rooting us in having been made in God's image and second by enabling us to see that others have also been made in God's image.

Read through the book of Ephesians (it's only six chapters). Highlight every verse in which Paul includes these phrases:

+ "in Christ"
+ "in him"
+ "with him"

Paul understood that *in Christ*, we are new creations (2 Corinthians 5:17). We may not feel it, know it, or believe it, but in God's eyes we have a new identity. Paul's letters to the Galatians, Philippians, and Colossians are equally rich resources for understanding Christian identity through our heavenly Father's eyes.

FINDING YOUR WINDOW:
MEALTIME, TRAVEL TIME, BEDTIME, AND MORNING TIME

> *Love the* LORD *your God with all your heart and with all your soul and with all your strength. These commandments that I give you today are to be on your hearts. Impress them on your children. Talk about them* **when you sit** *at home and* **when you walk** *along the road,* **when you lie down** *and* **when you get up.**
>
> DEUTERONOMY 6:5-7, *emphasis added*

"When you sit": Plan a family TV dinner and watch the Mister Rogers movie together.[9] Ask your kids to identify different ways he helped others with compassion and care. Discuss Mister Rogers's passion and approach. See if you can connect it to the *why* of your family's faith in Jesus and what it means to experience heaven here and now.

"When you walk": On your next commute, teach your kids the six ways the Holy Spirit operates. With each one, discuss what it could look like in class, at recess, on the bus, or with friends when no parents are around. Pray about each of these six ways the Holy Spirit operates, asking the Spirit to give your children eyes to see who needs extra care.

"When you lie down": At bedtime, read a chapter from Galatians, Ephesians, Philippians, or Colossians aloud. Ask your kids to say

"Ooh!" every time they hear one of the three phrases "in Christ," "in him," or "with him." Each time they stop you, ask your kids how God sees us according to the verse you're reading.

"When you get up": Over breakfast, talk about people who are struggling. Have your kids pray for people who are sick, are sad, are in need, just moved, or are out of work so they get used to going to the Lord in prayer.

DIY DISCIPLEMAKING ACTIVITY #5
Winter Coat Drive

JOIN OTHER FAMILIES and organize a winter coat drive in your driveway.[10] Explain that compassion is learning to see others' needs as simply different from your own. Some neighbors in your city might need warmer clothes as the season turns. (This activity works best before winter weather sets in.)

- Identify a local partner to help you redistribute what you collect. A foster-care ministry is ideal, or the Salvation Army often offers temporary accommodations to families. Maybe you have a teacher friend or know of a Title I–eligible school. A subsidized apartment facility might also be worth contacting.

- As a family and with a few friends, post yard signs, send out emails, and share about the coat drive on your neighborhood Facebook page, in an HOA email, or on the Nextdoor app. Invite neighbors and friends from your kids' schools to participate. Set out a table with coffee, doughnuts, and breakfast tacos.

- Gather your kids and community group beforehand to pray and talk about how *gospel* means "good news." Does warm clothing sound like good news on a really cold day?

Explain how if we plant the gospel in neighborhoods and with friends, the church will surely grow from it. Involve the kids in hospitality. Explain that they are hosts, and describe what that might look like as people drop by.

✿ The redistribution process for the gathered winter clothing will depend on whom you partner with, but to the extent that you're able, try to share the event with other families and especially your kids in hopes of them experiencing how God is using them to meet others' needs.

CHAPTER 6

A RHYTHM OF GENEROSITY

Sharing with Others What Already Belongs to God

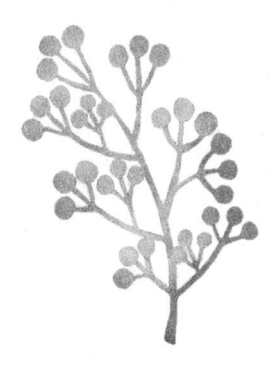

EVEN WHEN WE HAVE THE OPPORTUNITY to give money to people who need it, we will always have a sense that it's not enough. When our faith community gave away three thousand dollars to three nonprofits during The Pitch event, I'm sure the money was helpful to them—but we weren't changing the world. Don't we all feel helpless to bring noticeable change? None of us—no organizing agency and no amount of money—can heal broken creation. So where does that leave us as people with resources and concern for the vulnerable and marginalized in our cities? That's where a rhythm of generosity comes in.

We don't give to save anyone.

We give to save ourselves from believing we deserve what God has provided.

Parents reside on the giving side of the ledger throughout most of our kids' childhoods. Oh, we get paid with Velcro hugs, butterfly kisses, a captive audience to bad jokes, and, of course, naming rights—first, middle, and last. We are reimbursed with giggles from under the covers, the power to heal owies and scare away monsters under the bed, and the chance to be partners in flying kites and building sandcastles. We get to love our kids without limits so one day they might love without counting the cost.

> *We don't give to save anyone. We give to save ourselves from believing we deserve what God has provided.*

I cannot think of a better way for disciples to learn about God's generous nature than by raising kids. Parenting incarnates the selfless, giving nature of the God who loves.

Generosity saturates our relationships with grace. Like in parenting, our heavenly Father's grace is without limits but comes at a humbling cost. We grow in grace by understanding—in subtle and grand ways—that all we have is a gift from God. If we want to help our kids personally and affectionately encounter God, we will teach them about giving. We don't wait for them to have more to give but rather start with what they do have. Raising and discipling children can illustrate the generous ways God provides for and sustains us along the way.

THE UNFAIRNESS OF GRACE

One of life's earliest lessons for every kid is "It's not fair," which is code for "I'm not getting my way." Who doesn't keep a mental scorecard tied to personal justice and/or rewards? Maybe fairness—or lack thereof—has something to teach us about grace. At times, generosity is neither rational (as we'll see) nor fair. Fairness is always a slippery slope. Sometimes a situation favors us, and other times another person benefits. We're as likely to receive undeserved credit, gifts, and praise as we are to shoulder the blame or get the shaft.

In an unusual scene described in Luke's Gospel, Jesus is dining at the home of a Pharisee who seems to have invited an exclusive insider crowd. His guests jockey for the highest positions of honor at the table. In response, Jesus offers a lesson not just in hospitality but also in generosity:

> [Jesus said,] "When you give a luncheon or dinner, do not invite your friends, your brothers or sisters, your relatives, or your rich neighbors; if you do, they may invite you back and so you will be repaid. But when you give a banquet, invite the poor, the crippled, the lame, the blind, and you will be blessed. Although they cannot repay you, you will be repaid at the resurrection of the righteous."
>
> LUKE 14:12-14

To comprehend this command, it might be helpful to see ourselves in the second group of guests. Jesus welcomes those who have nothing to give and nothing to earn.

Apparently, when it comes to giving, Jesus isn't worried about payback!

Whether with friends, our spouses, our children, in business, or in what we expect of God, the scorecard system never adds up like we think it should. Nothing sounds more counterintuitive to what Jesus is saying to our hard-driving, bigger-is-better Western mindset.

But sacrifice isn't just helpful; it's necessary for human flourishing.

Suppose you think about the person you feel most indebted to and grateful for—the one who gave you the most, first believed in you, or invested in your education. The oddest thing we could try to do is repay them.

The only reasonable response to experiencing generosity, then, is to extend it to others.

Grace allows us to experience Christ's gift in the same way children receive loving gifts from their parents. Grace invites us to participate more deeply in the Kingdom without fearing being disqualified from God's love when we mess up.

Parenting can offer us a new way to understand and receive the Good News of Jesus. The gospel is the greatest, most joyfully enigmatic news anyone could ever hear. It is the ultimate expression of love. God Himself has saved us. In Him, we find our identity and belonging the same way our children find theirs in our families. But the gospel is often proclaimed with a teaspoon of joyfulness and several gallons of "Here's what you should do about it." That's not a proclamation of good news. That is replacing the Jewish law with a new Christian law, emphasizing what we do and robbing Christ of the glory of the spectacular thing He has done. A rhythm of generosity reminds us of what we've been freely given and that we need not keep receipts for what we give.

> *A rhythm of generosity reminds us of what we've been freely given and that we need not keep receipts for what we give.*

Discipleship involves constant wrestling with the tension of God being the Provider and *us* making the sacrifices, doing the heavy lifting, and assuming the credit. An award at the Oscars or the Olympics might reward one person's accomplishment, and the victory speech typically offers thanks to significant people who supported the winner's pursuits. But while those contributions were significant, what's not seen is how God provided for their success. Skill, coaching, passion, drive, technology, nutrients, talent, health—all the things that allow a person to excel at the highest level—are gifts. When we find ourselves on top, the subtle problem is that we can get lulled into believing that God wasn't part of the equation since we did all the work, took all the risks, and made all the sacrifices.

GRACE AS GENEROSITY

To experiment with grace and generosity, our family organized a weeklong initiative called Dime Store Philanthropy. With a few other families, we asked, "What would happen if we put ourselves in the shoes of a person who lives with a lot less?" We explained to our kids that we wanted to live more simply and give more generously. There are many readily available poverty statistics online; for our family, we explained that millions of people in the world live on about two dollars per day.[1]

Each night at dinnertime and bedtime, I'd share a Bible verse and/or a statistic about illiteracy, clean water, average income, or health care access. We're trying to do what Paul says in Colossians 3:12: "As God's chosen people, holy and dearly loved, clothe yourselves with compassion, kindness, humility, gentleness and patience." Or, in as another translation puts it, "put on a heart of compassion" (NASB), which means to suffer with those suffering.

The idea is simple: For one week, budget each dinner at two dollars per person. For instance, our family of four had an eight-dollar dinner every evening. It's tricky, but it can be done.

Walking through the grocery store aisles together, our family carefully looked at prices, creatively imagining what we could afford.

We found pasta and sauce, maybe mushrooms, but had to pass on adding meat.

And since much of the world lives on rice and beans, we added those to the menu too. This experiment in generosity meant planning meals and sticking to the plan.

One Tuesday evening, we finished a Little League game around dinnertime. I had both kids while Laurel was still at work. I suggested we stop at the drive-through on our way home but then remembered our plan. Even the minor inconvenience of delayed gratification and a less exciting diet made the principle hit home for our kids. The experience was gamelike to navigate, but it was helpful for them to practice giving of themselves to God and for a cause.

Of course, the fun part was pooling our resources to see how much money we'd saved. With that money, we purchased twenty-five-dollar grocery store gift cards. We agreed to find individuals in need, learn their names, and hear their stories. Several families participating in the experiment had great experiences, especially my friend Shannon, who took her three kids to a grocery store in a lower-income part of town so they could possibly, and prayerfully, meet someone who might need and receive their help.

This exercise taught us that generosity is not about who is deserving, faithful, responsible, or trustworthy, because in any given situation, the giver is as vulnerable as the receiver.

Viewing grace through our parenting eyes can reveal our gracious God as the Source of every good gift. Any parent can see how much they provide for and sustain their children even when kids think they're accomplishing something independently. It's the infant taking a few first steps while we guide their wobble. It's the child on a swing exclaiming, "Look how high I am!" while we push from behind. It's Little League success after countless hours of backyard batting practice or the recital dependent on our taxi service. It's them making the honor roll because we relearned math to tutor them. It's our kids making friends because we arrange playdates for them.

We hit the threshold of grace when we discover that all we have is a gift because there's a Giver.

THE COST OF GROWTH

A rhythm of generosity can hit us where it hurts, but I'm not simply referring to our bank accounts. In our consumerist culture, we're trained to think more is better. But no one ever explains the shadow side of widening, extending, deepening, and even insulating our lives with abundance.

When Jesus offers us the Lord's Prayer in Luke 11:2-4, His request for daily bread calls to mind when God fed the hungry Israelites daily in the desert. But He may also have had in mind a passage from Proverbs 30 that encourages us to ask God for *only* our daily bread.[2] The request for daily bread in the Lord's Prayer offers a commentary on our human tendency toward self-sufficiency, where we subtly forget to see God as the Source and forget to see how we might incarnate His gracious gifts. Living as if we don't need God is a steep price to pay for financial wealth.

The cost of growth is this: Every time we gain something, we lose something.

The cost of growth is this: Every time we gain something, we lose something.

When it comes to parenting, with every developmental transition our children go through, we experience loss. Our culture teaches us that we can have it all. Yet we only grow by letting go. In some cases, that means we grieve the loss of something at the same time something new begins.

Many changes happen to our kids. We blink, and they go from taking their first steps to having their first day of kindergarten. And before we know it, we start losing some of our influence over our children to their adolescent peers.

We experience a sense of loss when they obtain driver's licenses and miss some meals together at the family table.

And all too soon, we move them into a college dorm room and every night as we lock the front door are reminded, *They're not coming home tonight.*

All these developmental transitions are natural and what we want to see happen as we give ourselves to seeing our kids flourish. But growth requires loss, letting go. Things can't be like they were, but just like our heavenly Father does with us, we find new ways to give. This is one place God speaks to us through our kids.

Understanding that parenting involves loss can help us make sense of a curious exchange described in the Gospel of John: when Mary discovered that Jesus had risen from His grave.

> Jesus said, "Do not hold on to me, for I have not yet ascended to the Father. Go instead to my brothers and tell them, 'I am ascending to my Father and your Father, to my God and your God.'"
> JOHN 20:17

Mary had spent years traveling and working with Jesus. She'd watched Him die. She visited His grave, and when she recognized Him, she went in for a hug. And oddly, Jesus stopped her. It was His way of explaining that in this new season, it couldn't be like it once was. Parenting through developmental transitions can feel the same way. I remember holding Bjørn's hand as we approached his first-grade school. Suddenly, he did *the pullback*. It was the first time he pulled his hand out of mine. I was sad, but I could also see a transition unfolding. He wasn't just growing more aware of his peers but also growing up, becoming more independent. Do you remember when your kids did a pullback from you? It's not a rejection, but—like with Jesus and Mary—there's a transition unfolding.

TRUSTEES MORE THAN STEWARDS

It's hard to imagine being a part-time parent. Even when we aren't with our kids, we remain fully invested in their growth, wanting them to flourish. Have you ever thought that our kids aren't *our* kids but God's? He has entrusted the care of His children to us. He wants them to know Him, recognize His voice, and experience His love. They are ultimately not ours but His. We are not parent-owners but trustees. Parenting is learning to see all that we have and all that we are as a sacred trust. We are not owners, or even stewards. We are trustees.

An owner holds possession.

A steward manages their own assets and affairs.

A trustee manages what's *not* theirs. Trustees understand the nature of ownership differently. Disciplemaking becomes a sacred trust as we manage what's ours *and* God's.

As it relates to earthly possessions and resources, God is always the Source.[3] Trustees can never sell an estate, because it's not their own. They can take a percentage of its revenue for managing or administering the trust, but that's it. One problem with how Christians traditionally view tithing is that we forget that "the the earth is the Lord's, and everything in it" (Psalm 24:1), which means that the earth is God's estate. It's God's trust. We own nothing, and we prove it when we die: Our possessions remain behind.

A proper theology of tithing is not in giving but in receiving. A theology of receiving comes before giving. God made us to be receivers. This is the free and gracious gift of salvation in which we receive the King and His Kingdom.[4] If we take the view that all we have is a gift from God, then it's worth practicing—and giving our kids some imagination for—how to operate as divine trustees.

For several years, our faith community organized a faith experiment for the forty days of Lent. Jesus' death and resurrection promise new life, and not just once and for all: They give us the chance to be renewed often and as needed. The experiment was called A New Normal, because to experience any kind of reset, we need an interruption to our usual way of doing life. Many people use Lent as a time of fasting—from wine, chocolate, or social media. Ours was a family fast of a different kind.

We suggested to our community of families to try fasting daily from ordinary expenditures and keep a running total of what they might have spent but didn't during this time frame. These were simple savings that could involve kids and adults alike: choosing to drink water instead of expensive beverages when eating out, handwashing the car instead of taking it through the car wash, drinking office- or home-brewed coffee instead of grabbing Starbucks, packing a lunch instead of eating at the cafeteria, streaming movies at home instead of going to the theater. The point was to keep tabs on savings. On Palm Sunday, we all turned in our savings. A week later, on Easter Sunday, we held a small service where we passed out twenty-five dollars to each person with a charge to go and live into the Resurrection by bringing life to others.

Parenting exercises the generosity muscle. God wants to shape our giving of ourselves to His mission in the world. This vision is worth seeding in our kids' understanding and Kingdom imagination. Generosity isn't about how much I give but how much I'm embodying God as a "little Christ."[5] If we believe that every good and perfect gift comes from Him (James 1:17), wouldn't generosity be a way to bear that image to our kids? Practicing our faith by having a rhythm of generosity isn't about getting our names attached to scholarships or buildings because of sizable donations; it's about reflecting God's image.

NAME, IMAGE, AND LIKENESS

The concept of *name, image, and likeness* (NIL) has dramatically changed the financial landscape of college sports. The arrangement allows athletes to profit from use of their name, image, and likeness in endorsements, sponsorships, and other opportunities. Critics of NIL argue that the bidding wars involved exacerbate the rich getting richer. Others contend that student-athletes are entitled to share in the wealth they help generate. The receipts are staggering—not just how much programs pay for an eighteen-year-old's talent but also (even beyond their performance on the field) how much one player's social-media presence and overall marketability can earn.

As Christians, we have our own NIL agreement—but it's quite the opposite of the college-sports approach. It's not even about us. Instead, we bear the name, image, and likeness of God. In other words, we can become His incarnation in every culture and context. Being a Christ follower is not merely about securing a desired future for when our playing days are over. Our athletic abilities and social-media presence mean nothing for the Kingdom. It's how we bear the name, image, and likeness of God that truly matters.

THE ART AND SCIENCE OF GIVING

If we want to disciple our kids to reflect God's generous nature, it might also be helpful to understand the science behind giving. Whether in regard to finances, time, or effort, there's an important distinction between giving and spending, and the science behind these practices reveals God's heart.

When many people in our society spend money, it's typically for their own benefit and enjoyment. When researchers interviewed people about recent purchases, they found that spending money on other people, called "prosocial spending," boosts happiness (particularly when it's spent on things like group dinners or concerts rather than on material items, like shoes, electronics, or clothes). The *Journal of Happiness Studies* published a study exploring this topic: Participants recalled a previous purchase made for themselves or someone else and then reported their happiness at the time of purchase. Afterward, participants chose to spend a monetary windfall on themselves or someone else. Participants who recalled a purchase made for someone else reported feeling significantly happier immediately afterward.[6]

Most importantly, the happier participants felt, the more likely they were to choose to spend a windfall on someone else. So spending money on other people makes us happier than buying stuff for ourselves does. When it comes to giving our time and energy, research suggests that investing as little as that two hours per week in helping others can enrich our lives. Similar studies of volunteering reported similar findings.[7] In his book *Flourish: A Visionary New Understanding of Happiness and Well-Being,* Martin Seligman explains that helping others can improve our own lives: "We scientists have found that doing a kindness produces the single most reliable momentary increase in well-being of any exercise we have tested."[8]

The art of generosity and giving is discerning a need *and* being part of a response, even if it doesn't solve anything. When it comes to discipling our kids, God invites us to sow seeds and imagination, believing that, by faith, our kids will have giving hearts in light of God's provision.

In a confounding illustration of giving, Jesus allows a woman to "waste" an entire expensive fragrance bottle on him, saying, "The poor you will always have with you. . . . She did what she could" (Mark 14:7-8). God's love is lavish and even, at times, irrationally generous.

Yet God doesn't want our money—He wants us free.

If everything is a gift, then all that I have is not my own—family, friends, education, health, paycheck, clean drinking water—everything I have is an offering.

In fourth grade, our son began noticing that other families had more wealth than ours as well as bigger homes, club memberships, family ranches, second homes, nice cars, luxury trips, and paid help. While other families could outsource things, we cleaned our own home, did our own yard work, and washed our own cars. I explained to my son that we're building a life together. As a reminder of how rich we were in love through Christ, I often whispered to him, "Who's got it better than us?"[9] It was meant to shape a Kingdom perspective of gratitude. Our family was physically, emotionally, and spiritually present in the hard and the good, in labor and play. I wanted Bjørn not just to see what we did have but also to be content. I wanted him to see that God is active and generous.

We learn generosity by not waiting for the day when we have more. We grasp it by giving what we do have.

When Peter locked eyes with a beggar strategically positioned at the gates to the Temple where pious Jews came to pray, he didn't say, "Sorry, I have nothing to give you." He said, "Silver or gold I do not have, but what I do have I give you" (Acts 3:6). Generosity is as much about giving time as it is about money. It's about offering emotional support and human resources. This is what makes generosity so natural to instill in our kids. We're not asking them to write checks. We're teaching them how to give what they do have—because giving starts with knowing the Source of our gifts and having eyes to see how to demonstrate God's care in tangible ways. Generosity illustrates how God is giving to us as we give to our kids and others.

FINDING YOUR RHYTHM: EXPERIMENT WITH A NEW NORMAL

Try organizing your family to do experiments with generosity and grace. As I shared in this chapter, millions of people in the world live on about two dollars per day. Help your kids experience this reality. Plan a menu, go grocery shopping together, and discuss other ways that you could cut back on your daily expenditures.

Another experiment is practicing small sacrificial acts of fasting. The idea is to fast from regular purchases while keeping a running tab of your savings each week. With the savings, find opportunities to be generous in supporting people whose needs differ from your own. Lent is an ideal time, but this experiment can be done any time of year.

Creative Ways to Save Money from Our Daily Expenditures

Consider simple ways you can save money for a week. Keep a running total of how much you save from your usual spending habits and operating budget.

- Pass on Starbucks for office- or home-brewed coffee.
- Plan a dinner menu for the week and forgo the drive-through.
- Pack your lunch in lieu of eating out.
- Stream a movie instead of going to the theater.
- Wash your own car.
- Have a friend or spouse trim your hair.
- Change your car's oil yourself.
- Avoid impulse purchases at the checkout stand or gas station.

- If you eat out, opt for water instead of a fountain drink.
- Skip a meal.
- Avoid the snack bar or concession stand.
- Skip a round of golf, a happy hour after work, or an expensive outing.
- Buy sale items and store brands and use coupons to shop.

Creative Ways to Practice Generosity

- Host a dinner at a subsidized apartment complex where you eat alongside residents. Plan games for kids.
- Buy some fifty-dollar grocery store gift cards. Find a person at a streetlight looking for assistance. Learn their name and hear their story as you shop with them. Pray for them with your family.
- Connect with a local foster shelter or foster family. Ask about creative ways to encourage them.
- Use your proceeds to host a lake day, pool party, or Slip 'N Slide afternoon for refugee families or foster kids.
- Ask teacher friends if they know of any families facing food insecurity during the summer months.
- Identify a single-parent family. See if there's a way to help them afford something they might not otherwise enjoy (as you do, look for a way to make that parent shine in the eyes of their child).
- Invite your kids to discern a person with a concern and/or whom God might like to bless in a coffee, lunch, or dinner spot. Then anonymously buy them coffee or food.

FINDING YOUR WINDOW:
MEALTIME, TRAVEL TIME, BEDTIME, AND MORNING TIME

> *Love the* LORD *your God with all your heart and with all your soul and with all your strength. These commandments that I give you today are to be on your hearts. Impress them on your children. Talk about them* **when you sit** *at home and* **when you walk** *along the road,* **when you lie down** *and* **when you get up***.*
>
> DEUTERONOMY 6:5-7, *emphasis added*

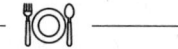

"When you sit": At the dinner table, read Colossians 3:11-13 aloud. Ask your kids what they think it means to "clothe yourselves with compassion, kindness, humility, gentleness and patience." When it says, "bear with each other," ask whose needs are different from your own and who might benefit from your family being generous in some way. It might help to google local or global statistics to illustrate the number of people around you who struggle to meet their basic needs.

"When you walk": During your next car ride, begin a discussion of why Jesus died for our sins. Did He have a choice? Did we deserve it? See if you can find the words to illustrate how grace and generosity work.

"When you lie down": Read Luke 14:12-14 and try to explain whom God wants us to be generous toward. Is it friends, people we know and like? Tell the story from Acts 3 of when Peter says to the man, "Silver or gold I do not have, but what I do have I give you" (Acts 3:6). What are the different ways we can give, and whom do your kids know with needs that differ from their own?

"When you get up": Assuming you organize your family to do one of the two faith experiments, begin to talk about the why, the need, and the opportunity. Ask, "Why do we fast?" (Christian fasting is purposefully giving up something we'd normally enjoy in hopes of gaining greater awareness of God's presence.) Pray for eyes to see what God sees and that He might invite you to be part of His response.

DIY DISCIPLEMAKING ACTIVITY #6
Walk a Mile in Their Shoes

OVER THE COURSE OF A WEEK, have each family member take a photo of someone else's shoes. It could be a classmate, neighbor, coworker, teacher, parent, boss, waitstaff member, or Uber driver. (It might be wise to ask permission before taking the picture.)

- Each night at dinner, share a picture of someone's shoes and describe how God gave you some insight into that person's life. Then imagine what it would be like to "go a mile in their shoes." What is it like to be them? What excites them? Worries them? Seek to gain their perspective. Listen for how God might speak to you or teach you about Himself and about others.

- Ask your kids how you might remember that individual by name and need in your prayers together.

- Talk to your kids about how empathy is critical for building compassion and generosity in our lives.

CHAPTER 7

A RHYTHM OF GRATITUDE

Showing Our Thanks in Big and Small Ways

IN ADDITION TO TAKING A FEW PICTURES, I recorded a written snapshot of Annika's sixth birthday in the journal I kept for her.

> You woke to unwrap a new outfit along with your favorite breakfast. You were recognized in front of the entire school at the morning assembly. We returned for lunch with Chick-fil-A, balloons, and cookies for the class. Everyone sang "Happy Birthday." You were the class line leader for the day. After dinner, Mom made a cake, we sang again, and you opened another gift. This time, an art easel! My favorite part was hearing you say, "I wish I could start this day all over again!" I wonder if that's how we're supposed to feel more of the time.

While we went all out today to help you feel special, it reminds me how God never stops feeling this way about us. Gratitude seems like it's in short supply. It doesn't always feel natural or easy, but I'm glad you got to experience it, if only for this day!

Have you ever noticed that reminding your kids to say thank you results in the most inauthentic gratitude? I'm not suggesting that having good manners and being thankful doesn't require training. But the universal prompt parents use when their child receives something ("What do you *saaaay*...?") leads to responses that inevitably feel forced.

It's not hard to spot the same kind of forced gratitude in adults who attend church. The leaders invite us to stand, sing, and worship as the service starts, so we do as they say. We declare God's worth because that's what we're expected to do in that setting. We know we're supposed to give thanks with a grateful heart (Colossians 3:15-16), but sometimes our responsibilities and pressure points weigh us down, making it hard for us to express thankfulness. And sometimes we're distracted from giving thanks because we're busy comparing ourselves to others, whom we perceive have more and better lives. We're created to worship, yet we're also wired with all kinds of emotions, some of which leave us decidedly *not* in a worshipful mood.

A rhythm of gratitude can help us move past circumstances and moods. A rhythm of gratitude is how every would-be disciple learns to "play" in God's Kingdom. This rhythm offers a gateway to wonder, joy, and celebration and helps us uncover simple pleasures. As we understand that every feeling is a gift from God—even the unpleasant ones—we can guide our kids to declare God's worth in grace and truth.

GRATITUDE AS A RAISE

In the well-known hymn "Come, Thou Fount of Every Blessing," we confusingly sing, "Here I raise my Ebenezer."[1] We're already standing, lifting our voices, and raising our hands. Now we've got an Ebenezer to raise too?

In all seriousness, many people don't know the meaning of *Ebenezer*, so allow me to help. *Ebenezer* comes from a Hebrew phrase meaning "stone of help."[2] In 1 Samuel 7, we read of the Israelites' fear of an encroaching Philistine army. As Samuel stood before the stone altar, "the LORD thundered with loud thunder against the Philistines and threw them into such a panic that they were routed before the Israelites" (1 Samuel 7:10). The *Merriam-Webster Dictionary* defines *ebenezer* as "a commemoration of divine assistance."[3]

We need divine memorials, artifacts, and heirlooms to remember God's assistance.

We need sanctified journals to recall God's faithfulness.

We need praise playlists to remind us of who God is despite any present circumstances.

We need incarnational iPhone photo albums to cherish the people who make God's love tangible for us.

We need family prayers layered with gratitude to reminisce about the big and small ways God shows up.

We raise an Ebenezer when we want to mark a story of God rescuing us. We might not feel like tuning our hearts to sing God's grace[4] in the moment—we might be at odds with a friend or facing a deadline or a health concern—but we're not limited to only giving thanks for the present. We worship God for His faithfulness throughout generations and our entire lives! And we all have Ebenezer stories of God redeeming us or providing for us. Since we're "prone to wander,"[5] I wonder if we notice all the times and ways God is saving, sparing, and rescuing us.

When Bjørn was three weeks old, he was diagnosed with a digestive condition called pyloric stenosis.[6] He needed immediate surgery to correct his inability to digest food. My wife and I had waited five years to have kids and experienced two miscarriages. We were unsettled by the thought of having our three-week-old son operated on, because we felt helpless. God had given us a son, and we could not care for him.

The procedure was successful, but the doctor informed us of a hernia, which would require another surgery the following week. He showed us a bulge protruding from our son's intestinal lining. We were disheartened.

After scheduling another surgery for our newborn, we drove home. All week, we prayed as only helpless parents can. On the day of Bjørn's procedure, as we were loading the car, we anointed and prayed over Bjørn one final time, saying, "Lord, will You mark his life from the earliest age as a testimony of Your healing mercies, care, and presence so that he might know You?" When we arrived at the hospital, were admitted, and found our room, medical personnel were parading in and out in preparation. All were pleasant and upbeat while inspecting our son, but no one offered information about his procedure. Then, finally, the doctor came in to explain that a second surgery was unnecessary. "We can't find anything wrong with your son. We had documented evidence of his hernia, but the imaging indicates there's nothing there to repair now."

How many stories of deliverance, close calls, and second chances have we failed to raise? I'm convinced there are more instances like this than we could imagine. But the small scar left from Bjørn's incision serves as a tangible reminder of God's healing. Like an Ebenezer—our "stone of help"—this scar under his belly button is a mark we've "raised" often to illustrate God's care and Bjørn's belonging to Him. This emblem of gratitude is how we've tried to shape his heart and mind with the reality of God's presence.

So, more than any forced thank you, what can parents practice "raising" with their kids? Gratitude is not always a knee-jerk reaction, but it can help us rise above culture's critique and our own (or our children's) unhappiness. Practicing gratitude can be a lot like trying to eat healthily: It's easy to indulge, but we feel more energized when we eat clean foods and moderate portions. Being grateful, and specifically giving God our praise, is a critical reframing rhythm.

Raise a glass at dinner to celebrate God's goodness. Cheers to that!

Raise your voice—sing loud and sing proud—to make known what Christ has done.

Raise your hands in applause and high fives to acknowledge Christ at work and God's name revealed.

Raise your hands in surrender to demonstrate your need, humility, and uncertainty. Invite your kids to cup their hands in prayer as both an offering and request.

Raise your pen to write sticky-note messages that boast of God's love for your kids, then place the notes in lunch bags and backpacks for your kids to find later.

MANAGING FEELINGS

As I illustrated in an earlier chapter, Fred Rogers saw children as vulnerable and believed that feelings could be mentioned and managed constructively. On his program, instead of pushing a political agenda, Fred Rogers was courageously vulnerable. He was willing to cross social divides and tackle issues of race, divorce, disabilities, and equality to help us understand a better way. He was full of faith, conviction, courage, and respect. Among many other qualities, Mister Rogers had the gift of poise—a high capacity for empathy, for nurturing children and expressing concern for them amid the struggles they experienced.

A rhythm of gratitude can help us reframe our feelings as gifts from God, who didn't create apathetic artificial intelligence but passionate beings who learn to feel what He feels. Created in the likeness of God, we are gifted the chance to not only feel how God feels but also respond in His name. I find it helpful to view our feelings—from pleasant to undesirable—as all rooted in God's heart. And if God designed us with this whole range of unique emotions and the capacity to feel, then it stands to reason He also has a healthy and life-giving way for us to express our feelings.

The idea that we should ignore our feelings is inhumane. There are appropriate levels of response for various circumstances, for sure. But too many people have learned to keep up a happy face to avoid being a burden or embarrassing themselves. Others never learned healthy boundaries for what should and shouldn't be expressed. Emotional filters are part of emotional intelligence, but using discretion about what we share and with whom is different from not feeling. We ought to find life-giving postures to honor God in our pain and joy, with our words and self-control, with our enthusiastic embrace and physical restraint.

For instance,

- When Jesus said, "Blessed are the peacemakers" (Matthew 5:9), He wasn't suggesting we should avoid problems or blind spots or ignore abuse or accusations.

- Finding comfort is not the same thing as numbing pain with a substance of our choosing.

- Anger compounded with physical violence and verbal attacks doesn't honor God. But anger expressed as advocacy, compassion, and justice does.

- A passionate impulse that's in service of another is life-giving, but erotic love and self-indulgence devalue life.

- Grief and sorrow help us cherish a loved one's impact. Even their absence reveals the Incarnation as a tangible way that God manifests His presence through people who bear His image.

The Exile is central to Jewish identity. The story reminds them of who they are—a delivered people. Just like money can enslave us, emotions can hold families captive. And yet God wants our hearts free to receive: to celebrate God and cherish the lives we have. But gratitude isn't automatic as much as it is cultivated and rehearsed.

Rehearsing a rhythm of gratitude—in the hard and the good—can deliver us from despair.

For families, there is no gratitude where there is no filter for what's appropriate to express out loud.

When our kids are having a hard time managing their emotions, we can take time to explain our expectation for attitudes. Asking them to "use their words" and "put away their tears" are sometimes helpful ways to minimize meltdowns. A common refrain in our house was "I can't help you if I can't understand what's wrong." But my wife and I also instilled consequences like cutting playdates short, postponing a visit to the toy store, or skipping dessert after dinner. This helped our kids learn that their

> *Rehearsing a rhythm of gratitude—in the hard and the good—can deliver us from despair.*

reactions could make us respond to their requests with a no. When families allow words and attitudes to be unfiltered and unaccountable, home will mostly feel like work and lack joy. And it's hard to feel grateful for God's abundance when we're overwhelmed by tantrums and back talk.

INSTILLING GRATITUDE AS MIRRORING

Every person's emotional self and physical being are fully integrated. Some are better at hiding their emotions than others, but most people reveal their feelings with physical responses. Kids naturally run to our embrace, celebrate dessert with arms raised, or smile and giggle at a puppy's lick bath. Our physical lives are equally intertwined with our spiritual lives. The affection we hold for God—our gratitude and desire—shouldn't be a mystery. Even when we don't feel close to God in a particular season, our physical response to His presence aligns our hearts and renews our minds to declare His worth.

One of the ways I coached our children was to mirror a person's greeting, especially with adults. If a person smiled at them, they should smile back. If they called them by name, looked them in the eyes, and/or shook their hand, they should mirror the adult's action and energy. Of course, I wanted our kids to be respectful. But I also wanted to help them with emotional intelligence. I asked how they might feel about these non-reactions:

- "How would you feel if you scored a goal but, instead of celebrating, your teammates yawned or began scrolling on their phones?"
- "How would you feel if you saw a grandparent you love but you weren't greeted with a smile and hug or called by name?"

- "How would you feel if you lost our dog, Posey, or a beloved toy and I just said, 'Oh well, we can find another one'?"
- "Imagine someone found a spider in bed with them but decided they were too tired to scream and just rolled over instead. How would you feel about that?"

These non-reactions make us cringe, right?!

The point is this: Our reactions to someone reveal how we feel about our relationship with them. And even if we don't feel emotionally close to someone, we want them to, in some small way, feel God's love through us when we interact with them.

These same intentional expressions and postures of gratitude are an important way to help our kids connect with God. Worship is learning to express our love, need, hope, and desire for God. If we believe that God is good, is present, cares, and forgives, then our love and affection for Him should never remain a secret. We don't have to be good singers to "make a joyful noise" (Psalm 98:4, KJV). God created our hearts and bodies for outward expression. In fact, the word *enthusiasm* comes from two Greek words, *en*, meaning "in," and *theos*, meaning "God."[7] It can be translated as "God within."

Gratitude is rooted in God, who celebrates life, beauty, truth, and goodness. We lift our voices so the rocks don't have to.[8] We clap in celebration or raise our hands in surrender. We bow our heads in respect. We close our eyes to focus or imagine. We stand in awe and kneel in humility. All these postures are ways we show how we feel and what we believe. In his book *Beholding*, spiritual director Strahan Coleman offers, "Theology is essentially theory until it meets the real-life decisions of our active lives, and the New Testament calls our *bodies* 'temples of the Holy Spirit,' not our *brains*."[9] Hearts feel, and the physicality of giving thanks in worship is a convergence of head, heart, and body. It's a valuable way we disciple our kids to integrate and root their lives in faith. The one thing we don't want to do, in any setting, is hide our gratitude.

PLAYING WITH GRATITUDE

Parenting can be both serious business and a sandbox to play in. Like faith, parenting is more art than science. It's more mystery than certainty, stillness than striving. Perhaps it might help to approach spiritual leadership with more fun than fear. A rhythm of gratitude flows out of the relationship we have as beloved sons and daughters of God.

There's something about playing hooky that makes any day seem like more of an adventure if not more fun. When you feel like you're getting away with something, it makes your smile a wee bit wider. With the school year winding down, most final days are filled with class parties, dress-up days, classroom cleanups, and end-of-the-year celebrations. One year, as a parent with a mild case of FOMO, I didn't want my kids' teachers and school friends to have all the fun.

A rhythm of gratitude flows out of the relationship we have as beloved sons and daughters of God.

With third and fifth grade winding down, we did our usual morning ritual that day. Wake up at 6:15 a.m., shower, make peanut butter toast at the kitchen counter, make lunches, pack bags, and do all this while watching the clock to be out the door by 7:30 a.m. You'd think we'd have had it down by now, but without fail, we'd still find ourselves repeating the same reminders and hustling to get out the door. This day was no exception—except that Laurel and I had made additional preparations. Thankfully, we live about two minutes—driveway to driveway—from the school. But like at any school, drop-off is a rush hour with many pedestrians to look out for.

As we approached the drop-off parking lot, I feigned distraction and added frustration to my voice as I rolled past the driveway.

"Oh man, I missed it! I got distracted. Ugh!" The kids replied, "Dad, we're gonna be late!"

"I know, but let me just circle the block and come back."

"We won't have enough time."

With the school in the rearview mirror and the highway in front of us, I said, "Should we just skip it?"

"Wait. What? Dad, are you serious?"

I replied, "Maybe we should just go to Schlitterbahn instead..." (For those unaware: Schlitterbahn is a massive water park, a guaranteed-fun family memory maker!)

Few moments in a parent's life are as treasured as the fleeting years of childhood and adolescence. As I suggested this unfairest of trades—school for the water park—unbridled celebration gave way to high praise for how great of parents we are (at least in the eyes of our kids and in this moment, but I'll take it). And that was before we stopped for doughnuts!

Have you heard of the priesthood of all believers? This is an essential Christian doctrine that suggests that every believer has the means to put the divine on display. We do more than fill volunteer roles at church for programs; we are image bearers who are called out to reflect God's likeness to the world, regardless of whether we're bishops or barbers, priests or a stay-at-home parents.

Similar to being part of the priesthood of all believers, parents who are raising homegrown disciples can also be part of God's *arthood* of all believers.[10] The arthood of all believers celebrates curiosity, awe, and wonder. As image bearers of God, we reflect the

Creator's design for play and passion. Seriousness, certainty, and busyness become the cancer that spreads and robs many of us of generativity and thankfulness. Against cultural norms, Jesus not only celebrated the presence of children but also invited us all to become like them.

For parents who wrestle with fear and anxiety about their children's safety, health, social standing, and/or upward trajectory, it might be helpful to let God incarnate His presence by embodying the more trusting temperament of a child. Imagine growing old and becoming like a child. Jesus said, "Unless you change and become like little children, you will never enter the kingdom of heaven" (Matthew 18:3). (This makes me wonder if there will be any grown-ups in heaven.) We might have to teach kids social cues to be polite and give thanks, but children always take the lead with unfiltered and authentic responses of joy, wonder, and creativity. This is important because God wants to do new work and renew creation. Disciplemaking should always arc toward renewing heaven on earth. The King is returning, so we need childlike imagination to participate in God's re-creation, rebuilding, and restoring of paradise.

AN IDENTITY WORTH CELEBRATING

I don't know many young parents who are morning people. And the idea of getting any time alone, especially with young kids, is like the psalmist crying out to God, "Where can I go . . . from your presence?" (Psalm 139:7). The presence of family, their unpicked-up remnants in each room, and the weight of deadlines and to-dos make finding the Lord at the beginning of a day seem like as much of a fantasy as sleeping in.

But taking time throughout the day to remember our identity in Christ helps us have gratitude toward God. Especially when parenting is draining us of our energy or when we are wrestling with God in our brokenness, remembering who we are in Christ—not what we have achieved—will shift our perspective. We are created in God's image, and so are our children!

In Genesis 32, Jacob wrestles with God all night. He's already established a reputation as a deceiver, and now, with his life in jeopardy, he's at a breaking point. It's like he's finally taking a long look in a mirror and wrestling with who he is. At the climax of this heavyweight fight, this conversation stops Jacob in his tracks:

> The man asked him, "What is your name?"
>
> "Jacob," he answered.
>
> Then the man said, "Your name will no longer be Jacob, but Israel, because you have struggled with God and with humans and have overcome."
>
> . . . So Jacob called the place Peniel, saying, "It is because I saw God face to face, and yet my life was spared."
>
> The sun rose above him as he passed Peniel, and he was limping because of his hip.
>
> GENESIS 32:27-28, 30-31

After the wrestling match, Jacob is renamed Israel (which means "someone who struggles with God"), and to celebrate his new identity, he names the location of this life-changing encounter with God. Israel's experience brings to light some truths for all believers:

Through Christ, we all have new names and a new identity. The idea of being reborn, renamed, and reshaped is worth the struggle. Being children of God means we are closer to God than we realize: We have direct access to the Father.

Like Jacob, we're all blessed by a limp. It's our frailty, not our strength, that helps us encounter God. A "limp" is a limitation that allows us to see God face to face. We live in a world that wants to exploit our inadequacies and expose the undeveloped strengths in our children. But our Christian identity reminds us not just *who* we are but *whose* we are.

Rather than raise overachievers or instill a false sense of self-confidence in our kids, we can celebrate their desires and efforts more than the results and outcomes. We can also celebrate who we are as image bearers rather than focusing on our achievements and failures. We rally around God's grace, which says we're already enough, we're loved, and we belong.

GROUNDED IN TRUTH

During an actor's strike, I read that it's better to be an unemployed screenwriter than an unemployed actor. If you're an out-of-work screenwriter, if someone doesn't buy your script, the rejection is toward your work. But if you're an actor, if someone doesn't buy your acting, the rejection is toward you. This illustration captures a tension many people wrestle with: trying to separate *who we are* from *what we do*.

One of the valuable ways parents can disciple their children toward gratitude is by helping them understand the names of God. These names represent God's unchanging and timeless nature. God's names are static nouns, but we can think of them as dynamic verbs because God acts in the world and in our lives.

The Bible describes God using many different names (see a list of some of them in the "Finding Your Rhythm" section in this chapter); some of the more common names include Healer, Provider, Strong Tower, Redeemer, Savior, Counselor, and

Deliverer. In a culture that sees truth as relative and perception as reality, teaching the names of God is a simple but significant way we can disciple our children toward familiarity with God's absolute truths. Knowing the names of God also grounds disciples amid culture wars and personal storms.

One way the Bible reveals God's character and unchanging nature is by sharing His various names—and these names are a means by which we can experience God in personal ways. What's more, these names are meant to be experienced personally. God is not a static being but a dynamic relational presence in our lives. The Hebrew idea of knowing is not primarily cognitive but relational.[11] When we understand the names of God, we will better understand the person of God and grow in our ability to share His love with others.

As we encounter the grandeur of God personally, His names become our story. His truth becomes our truth.

FINDING YOUR RHYTHM: CALLING ON THE NAMES OF GOD

Learning the names of God gives us deep roots that ground us in truth and gratitude. The nature of God is unchanging, regardless of circumstance. Just as a thesaurus can expand our vocabulary, the names of God can help put words to how we sense and call on God. We should talk with our kids about these names, giving examples of how God has revealed the aspects of His character represented by these names. With each name, we have a deeper understanding of God's presence. With each experience, we discover more ways to worship and praise Him.

Read the following list of names for God. Take time to think about the implications of each name—amazingly, all these things are true! If you like, review the Scripture passage(s) associated with each (perhaps in multiple translations). Then answer the questions that follow.

HOMEGROWN DISCIPLES

My Advocate (1 John 2:1)	My Portion (Psalms 73:26; 119:57)
My Shepherd (Psalm 23:1; 1 Peter 5:4)	My Savior (Psalm 38:22)
My Deliverer (Romans 11:26)	My Strength and Defense (Isaiah 12:2)
The Father of Compassion (Psalm 86:15; 2 Corinthians 1:3)	The One Who Refreshes (Psalm 23:3)
God of Comfort (2 Corinthians 1:3)	The Potter (Isaiah 64:8)
The God Who Sees (Genesis 16:13)	My Provider (Genesis 22:14)
The God of All Grace (1 Peter 5:10)	The Lord Is Peace (Judges 6:24)
The God of Hope (Romans 15:13)	My Refiner and Purifier (Malachi 3:3)
The God Who Gives Endurance (Romans 15:5)	My Resting Place (Jeremiah 50:6)
Immanuel (Matthew 1:23)	The Resurrection and the Life (John 11:25)
The Lord Who Heals (Exodus 15:26)	My Strong Tower (Proverbs 18:10)
The Life-Giving Spirit (1 Corinthians 15:45)	My Shelter from the Storm (Isaiah 25:4)
The Light of the World (John 8:12)	My Shield (Deuteronomy 33:29)
My Mediator (1 Timothy 2:5)	My Salvation (Hebrews 5:9)
My Fortress (Psalm 18:2)	The Spirit of Justice (Isaiah 28:5-6)
My Glory (Psalm 3:3)	The Way, Truth, and Life (John 14:6)
My Helper (Hebrews 13:6)	Wisdom (Proverbs 8:12)
My Victory (Exodus 17:13-15)	My Counselor (Isaiah 9:6)
My Hope (Psalm 71:5; 1 Timothy 1:1)	My Redeemer (Isaiah 59:20)

A RHYTHM OF GRATITUDE

1. Which of these names of God have you personally encountered since you became a parent? As you list them, try to connect the name of God with an event or season of life where God has revealed His presence.

2. Are there any names you feel are hard to trust, accept, or encounter? What do you think might be behind this?

3. What are two or three of God's names that you want to pray over your children and help them understand in this season of their lives?

4. In meditating on this list of names, what faces come to mind of people who seem to embody certain names or attributes of God? (List each name alongside one of the names of God in the list.)

5. How have you seen one of these names reflected in your spouse?

6. In each of your children?

7. In the life of a parent or a godly mentor?

8. In the life of a friend in your community of parents?

9. As you give thanks to God for making Himself known, take time over dinner, on a phone call, or even in a text message to speak this revelation over each person listed above.

FINDING YOUR WINDOW:
MEALTIME, TRAVEL TIME, BEDTIME, AND MORNING TIME

> *Love the* LORD *your God with all your heart and with all your soul and with all your strength. These commandments that I give you today are to be on your hearts. Impress them on your children. Talk about them* **when you sit** *at home and* **when you walk** *along the road,* **when you lie down** *and* **when you get up.**
>
> DEUTERONOMY 6:5-7, *emphasis added*

"When you sit": At the dinner table, explain how each of God's names reveals an aspect of who God is. Then take turns sharing how you see an aspect of God's nature in the lives of each of your family members.

"When you walk": On a car ride or road trip, single one person out and take turns identifying ten ways you're grateful for them.

"When you lie down": At bedtime, ask your children, "What hard things are you grateful for?" These could be activities or experiences that are uncomfortable or challenging. Be ready to go first and give an example. Identify how God has redeemed things that have been unfortunate, difficult, or disappointing for good.

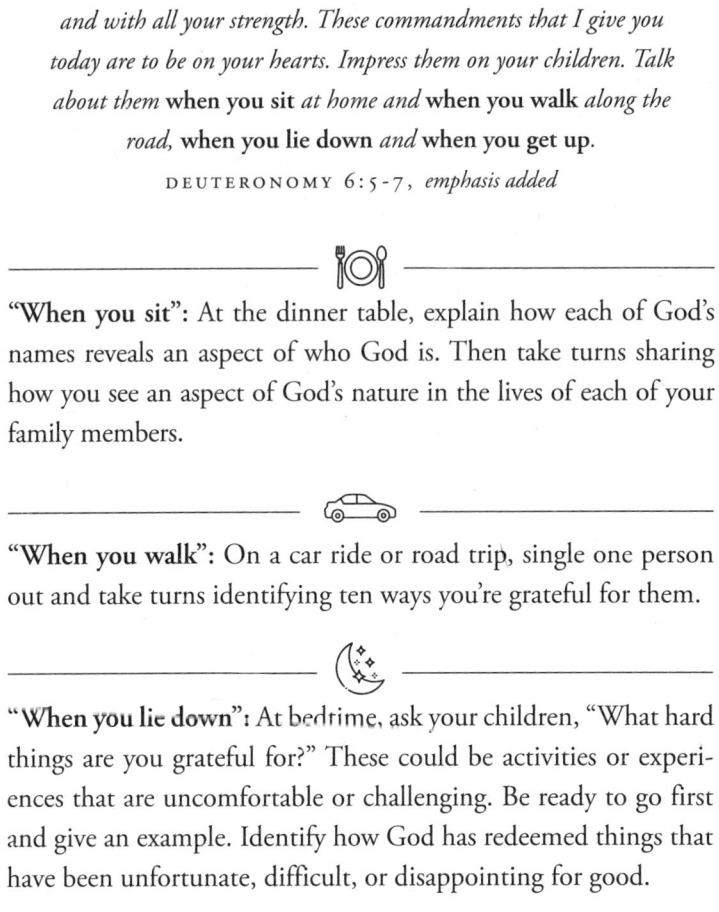

"**When you get up**": Encourage your kids to think of a time they encountered God in the last week. Be prepared to share a time you recently met God as well. Try to attach one of the names of God to bear witness to this revelation, and encourage your kids to do the same. What are you grateful for about these encounters?

DIY DISCIPLEMAKING ACTIVITY #7
Family Gratitude Journal

FOR A MONTH, during times you are gathered, talk about what each family member is grateful for. If you can, write these things down in a physical journal. Gratitude is a muscle worth exercising! Try not to repeat yourselves; think of new things each time.

But don't stop there. See if you can attach one of the names of God to each thing you write down. Knowing the names of God helps ground us in the truth of who God is, regardless of how we feel in a given moment or season. Remember that you're trying to illustrate the truth that God is constant, good, and relatable. After a month, review your family gratitude journal together and celebrate how long the list is!

CHAPTER 8

CROWNED AND COMMISSIONED

CROWNING IS BOTH an achievement and a beginning. An achievement feels like an arrival, and a beginning suggests a new chapter. Crowning happens at the births of babies and the coronation of monarchs. We crown athletes as champions, while artists and writers consider Academy Awards or Nobel Prizes their crowning achievements.

The Bible, too, illustrates how we are crowned: "You have made [humans] a little lower than God, / And You crown [us] with glory and majesty!" (Psalm 8:5, NASB). "The naive inherit foolishness, / But the sensible are crowned with knowledge" (Proverbs 14:18, NASB).

The crowning achievement of every parent occurs as we reproduce the life of Jesus in our children. We can't help but try to give our kids every advantage and opportunity to flourish. An inheritance is what we leave *for* our children, but a legacy is what we leave *in* them.

Being coronated by the Spirit of God to disciple is both an achievement and a beginning. The journey starts, even if we've been on this ride all our lives. With so much yet to learn, you still have much to impart, explain, and instill in your children. I am convinced that families contribute to a person's faith flourishing even more than the most positive of church experiences. The spiritual vitality of families covers a multitude of church shortcomings. That's why we need homegrown disciples. Parents who heed the call to be the lead disciplemakers, the primary spiritual leaders, in their children's lives: Let the church echo our desire for our kids to know Christ.

Throughout this book, I've sought to stir your imagination for spiritual reproduction—life begetting life by the seeds we sow. I've tried to inspire parents to discover incarnational faith rhythms to be ambassadors of heaven on earth. Like gardeners tilling the soil of our family lives, we seed how we put our trust in God so that our kids might also put their trust in Him. Of course, like growing any relationship, disciple seeding takes time, tending, and trust that God is working to bring and renew life.

NONARRIVAL

As we wrap up, we need to talk about arrival. Here's the most important thing to understand: Scripture doesn't include the concept of arrival!

You can get saved, but that's only the beginning!

We're invited into relationship, which remains fluid.

We're beckoned into sanctification, which is dynamic.

There's no retirement in the Kingdom of God.

And language matters. When we use phrases like *being a believer* or *being a convert*, we imply boxes that can be checked—you've arrived! Giving our mental consent to believe in God doesn't invite any reorientation of our lives. But, as James writes in his epistle, "even the demons believe [that there's one God]—and shudder" (James 2:19). The reason it's important to highlight this is because every Christian, if we're honest, is likely to admit that whatever stage of life we're in, we thought we'd be further along by now. We've attended church faithfully, said yes to many volunteer roles, led small groups, gone on mission trips, sat on committees, and even been close friends with pastors. Yet we're all left with a gnawing feeling of being spiritually underwhelmed.

And rather than letting this underwhelm create a longing and hunger for righteousness in us, many of us see our shortcomings more than our belonging.

Many people feel underwhelmed by the promises and presence of God rather than behold the relational God of both mystery and intimacy.

What's more, too many Christians never feel like they know enough or are good or confident enough to disciple others.

This is one of the great carcinogens plaguing the Western church today. We've allowed the narrative of inadequacy to keep us from Jesus' mission of making disciples who make disciples.

My prayer is that you will trust what heaven has revealed about who God is, not what hell's revealed to you about who you are not. Do the soul-searching and wordsmith work to discover the difference Christ is making in you. Allow the Spirit to reveal the timeline of God's faithfulness in your life and how He's provided for you and redeemed your broken places.

Parenting is the most Jesus-y disciplemaking enterprise imaginable. Our homes are the ideal soil for germinating God's grace, compassion, and sacrificial love. Jesus' invitation is to follow Him not at a distance but in proximity and tenderness. And, since walking in the Holy Spirit is often more caught than taught, kids need to experience the Spirit abiding in us as we yield to His prompts, explain our convictions, own our mistakes, and live out of God's abundance. God chooses every parent to reproduce their life spiritually not because we always get it right but because we know we need Him.

A helpful illustration I often use for how our spiritual unarrival works is twelve-step recovery. In case you're not familiar with this model: Step one is admitting you have a problem and can't overcome it alone. Sobriety happens in community. The next ten steps are about turning to God and making amends for all the hurt and harm caused because the addiction has spoken louder than one's intentions.

But the genius of the twelve-step program is something tied to step twelve: sponsorship.

Even though the person in recovery still has further to go, more to learn, temptation to battle, labor to do to remain sober and heal relationships . . . the way to work out their sobriety is to find someone at step one. If the church could work out our salvation like a person fighting addiction works out their sobriety, I believe it would transform lives from the inside out! Recovery isn't about buildings or budgets any more than the church is about platforms and programs. Both are relational movements in which people have realized what it means to survive, sustain, redeem, and recover.

Disciples aren't mass-produced. They're handcrafted. And this is what you're already doing.

"USE MY VOICE TILL YOU FIND YOURS"

I rely on the words of Jesus for the courage and confidence to live the life I'm called to live but am not able to live on my own. While my life is imperfect, my identity is secure, so I walk in His truth.

Whenever our children were battling nerves about tryouts, navigating schoolyard drama, preparing for presentations, owning their faith at school when it cost them greater acceptance, writing college-application essays, making difficult-but-right decisions to break up, or interviewing for jobs, like any parent, I'd try to offer insight and advice. But when I could see they still lacked courage, confidence, or conviction, I often used these words: "Use my voice till you find yours."

This is the voice of a disciplemaker. Parents have the most privileged place not only to see but also to speak to the insecurities of their kids. Many parents live vicariously through their children, which is not what I'm suggesting. This is not about projecting our desires onto them but about revealing God's desires, truth, acceptance, and relentless love for them. The world's messaging crowds out God's truth like a gravitational pull, making it a wonder we have any spring left in our step. Too often, we forget who we are in light of who Christ is. Like Jesus, who advocates on our behalf before His Father and gives us His power and authority to make disciples in His image, parents get to be that voice that says, "Use my voice till you find yours." It's in finding and giving voice to the reality of God that our kids can experience His presence.

I would also like to say the same thing to every Christian parent who lacks the courage, strength, or confidence to see themself as a disciplemaker.

As a fellow parent, my hope is that you will uncover all the ways God's Spirit is germinating in you. Any good fruit is worth sharing, and its seeds are worth planting. Disciplemaking is a time of germination—us in communion with Christ and our kids in fellowship with us. It involves figuring out what grows in your context and how much light and watering is required.

Culture is information biased, which keeps us from being incarnation based.

But in disciplemaking, *you* are the syllabus, and *your life experience in Christ* is the curriculum to impart.

Programs, books, information, volunteering, advice giving, and sacraments don't disciple people. They can contribute to spiritual growth. But only people can spiritually reproduce disciples because only humans carry the breath of God. Since Christians are already oriented to grow in knowledge, help in some capacity, give of their resources, and seek community life, I'm looking to inspire a more intentional developmental process than this that commissions parents to invest in what they already have. Disciplemaking not only shapes one more and more into God's image; it also involves learning how to reproduce that growth in others.

Remember, you already have God's Spirit in you. We don't create new life without God's Spirit as an animating life force. We can grow in the Spirit, but all life begins with the Creator.

Every parent is already engaged in the process of disciplemaking. Whether we mean to or not, we teach what we know and reproduce who we are.

Sometimes we reproduce our fears, prejudices, cynicism, desire for control, and lack of trust. But hopefully we will reproduce the hope, grace, healing, and love we have experienced in Christ.

The crisis of the church's collective faith is that most Christians lack the imagination to reproduce their faith. I want to move the goalposts to making disciples beyond salvation, baptism, acts of service, Bible knowledge, and good behavior. Programmatic Christianity is a helpful way to scale instruction for various size groups and life stages, but it's also the thing that emasculates Christians and keeps them from reproducing their faith. Rather than feeling prepared to invite people to shadow us, we're mostly spiritually equipped to invite people to church. Don't get me wrong; that's a great first step, but God calls us to much more. Producing homegrown disciples is about forming a relational covenant with our children to reveal, reproduce, and commission them to do likewise with others. Again, this is why parents are best suited for making disciples. No one knows your child better than you nor has more exposure, opportunity, and influence to instill a living faith in them.

Disciplemaking wasn't just central to Jesus' time on earth. It's central to how we experience the life of Christ. He didn't come for the masses as much as He came to train the few to reach the many. Upon Jesus' ascension, this earthly strategy was entrusted to those who bear His name. But rather than create a ministry in which to grow comfortable, familiar, and old together with the disciples, Jesus invested every bit of Himself, knowing He'd have to let them go out into the world. This is what makes this process so real for parents.

Life is learning to love what you know you'll lose.

Learning to love and learning to let go is an amazing part of life! Our hearts have been created with an unimaginably expansive quality. If you have multiple kids, prior to the arrival of each one, you probably couldn't imagine having the bandwidth to love more than you already did. But then they entered your life, and your bandwidth increased. God invites us to give our whole selves so that we can release and surrender that which has a hold on us. Giving away is not only a chance to reflect God's nature and participate in His redeeming work in the world, but it also helps us continue to see God as the Source of every good and perfect gift (James 1:17). And the God who has graciously provided for us up until now is the same God who will sustain us going forward.

Life is learning to love what you know you'll lose.

THE PROBLEMS WE PRAYED FOR

Have you heard the saying about raising kids that "the days are long but the years are short"? I often remind myself, *These are the problems I prayed for*. Parenting is good, whether it means experiencing sleep deprivation, losing Saturdays to kids' activities, or having less discretionary spending. Surrendering these things feels like the opposite of growing, but this is the relational and spiritual arc toward flourishing in the way of Jesus. Submitting what we cherish or rely on allows King Jesus to remain on the thrones of our hearts. This process is like pruning a rosebush to blossom again. We're dying to rise again. Parenting means less of me and more of Him. It tests the mettle of our identity and belonging. And God uses our children to reveal His love and shape us into His likeness.

Our surrendering is the means by which God continues His work in our kids. We train them to be independent, and then they emerge as capable and confident, holding their own convictions. Their independence also means less dependence on us as parents. Again, this is good news. Every season of parenting brings a new wrinkle, whether or not we (or our kids) are ready. Every season is worth celebrating and grieving. I have tried to embrace this tension as an act of faith. In cherishing, we remember how even when something feels like a loss, the resurrection of Jesus means that God can bring new life in it. The Resurrection promises that Jesus has risen and is rising, reigning, and returning. God wants to do new work, but it begins with letting go.

CORONATION AS COMMISSIONING

After moving Bjørn into college, we drove the two hours back to Austin with him to grab a few last things, say goodbye to friends, and have a final night at home. In the morning, I climbed into bed with him. Bjørn was excited and nervous to begin this new chapter. I was, too, but letting go felt like slipping on an undersized turtleneck, with threads of loss and sadness woven tightly around my neck. My joy was choked, but not my confidence in my son or my faith in the Father.

What transpired was a spontaneous and divine verbal stream of consciousness, like a pleasant dream you don't want to wake from. As we were lying there staring at the ceiling, Bjørn offered what every parent longs to hear: "Dad, so many kids keep saying how excited they are to get away from their parents and be on their own. But that's the last thing I feel."

I was overwhelmed, wanting to let his verbal affirmation linger in the air. It felt sacred. With tears in my eyes and a cracking voice, I began thanking him for being my son and affording me the best childhood a dad could wish for. He was a gracious gift that made my wife and I look like way better parents than we really were. Bjørn had an idea of who he wanted to be, even if it wasn't a popular one. God used him to be an encouragement to me, especially in pastoral ministry. (I still have the Post-its that he wrote at nine years old taped to my closet mirror: "Don't stop teaching people about God" and "You're a great writer.")

In a world that runs at a breakneck pace with on-demand expectations, some things should not be experienced in a hurry. Things like sipping wine, sunrises and sunsets, lovemaking, the last season of *Better Call Saul*, and—most certainly—childhood should be savored, not rushed.

Pausing for a breath, composing myself while cherishing this moment of apparent loss, I felt God give me an image of the Resurrection. I tried to describe to my son how up until now, I'd been able to contribute and be part of his spiritual, academic, athletic, and relational life. This next season would be life-changing. Of course, my wife and I would support, pray for, listen to, and visit our son, but this would be a transformational season, and we could only watch at a distance. I explained how he'd have to decide who he wanted to be, how he wanted to live, and whom he'd surround himself with. From personal experience, I knew this would be hard and lonely at times, but the Lord would meet and sustain Bjørn. The Resurrection confronts all of us, not only in the present day but with His presence today!

I knew this next season would feel dark, uncertain, lonely, unfamiliar, and even impossible at times. And yet I wanted to challenge Bjørn—and every Christian—with the belief that God can meet us when we're most vulnerable and alone and bring new life. Things can be both hard and good at the same time. The world's message is that what's easy is good and hard is bad. But that's largely untrue. As I tried to communicate to my son in that moment, God wants to do new work in him as much as in me. And as He does, we will experience Him in a new and transformational way.

RESURRECTING AND REPRODUCING

In the musical *Godspell*, Jesus dies in the finale rather than being resurrected.[1] The cast is typically directed to lift His body over their heads and walk off through the audience to end the show. Over the years, some critics have commented about the show's apparent lack of a Resurrection. Some view the curtain call, in which Jesus appears, as symbolic of the Resurrection; others point to the moment the cast raises Jesus above their heads.

While either view is valid, both miss the point. *Godspell* is about forming a community that carries on Jesus' teachings after He has gone. In other words, the effect Jesus has on the others is the story of the show, not whether He is resurrected. In Old English, *Godspell* comes from the words *god* (meaning "good") and *spell* (meaning "a story that has power"). As Christ's followers, we are called to do more than just believe in God; we are invited to operate under the power of the Good News. Jesus announced that all power and authority given to Him is given to us (Matthew 28:18-20; Luke 9:1). Jesus crowns us to live under "God's spell" in giving this life away.

Now Laurel and I find ourselves with young adult children. We're immeasurably bonded, inspired, and humbled by how the Spirit is alive in them. Our son, Bjørn, is an engineer working in renewable energy. Annika has begun her career as a NICU nurse. Both see themselves as image bearers and "sent ones" who put the divine on display. They're now investing their lives in specific children, youth, and couples. But this could only happen because of Jesus' modeling of the truth that life is learning to love that which you know you'll lose. I share these updates not as a humblebrag but rather as a testimony of God's grace and a revelation of Christ in them. They've come of age as citizens of heaven on earth, mindful of who they are and to whom they belong.

A verse I cling to says, "The student is not above the teacher, but everyone who is fully trained will be like their teacher" (Luke 6:40). Oh, whew! We don't have to make our kids better, brighter, or more spiritual than us! We simply mirror the life of Christ, who's already active and at work in us.

Psychologist Adam Grant comments, "Good teachers introduce new thoughts, but great teachers introduce new ways of thinking. Collecting a teacher's knowledge may help us solve the challenges of the day, but understanding how a teacher thinks can help us navigate the challenges of a lifetime."[2] Seeing our children come of age—despite having less time with and dependence on us—is the problem we prayed for. The fact is that our grown kids still need us but in different ways. And they do return as caring adults, allies, confidants, and colaborers in restoring heaven on earth.

My prayer is that you will see yourself as crowned and commissioned by the King for the Kingdom: crowned to reproduce Jesus in you and commissioned to participate in restoring the Kingdom God intended from the beginning.

Notes

INTRODUCTION | PARENTS AS DISCIPLEMAKERS
1. The Avett Brothers, "Murder in the City," track 2 on *The Second Gleam*, Ramseur Records, 2008.
2. For more on the meaning of this word in the original language and its occurrences in the Bible, see Blue Letter Bible, "Lexicon: Strong's H6005—'immānû'ēl," accessed July 19, 2024, https://www.blueletterbible.org/lexicon/h6005/niv/wlc/0-1.
3. See, for example, Matthew 4:19; 8:22; 10:38; 16:24; 19:21; Luke 5:27; John 1:43; 12:26; 21:19, 22.
4. Practicing Jews recite the Shema in modern times as well. For more on the Shema, see Tim Mackie, "What's the Meaning of the Jewish Shema Prayer in the Bible? Learning to Listen to and Love God," BibleProject, May 26, 2017, https://bibleproject.com/articles/what-is-the-shema.
5. Many insightful leaders have been keen to highlight these daily windows when teaching parents. My introduction to these windows came through my mentor, Tim Elmore, who was a key volunteer at KidStuf ministry at North Point Church in the 1990s. As a generational and leadership expert, Tim later wrote about it in one of his books: Tim Elmore, *Nurturing the Leader Within Your Child: What Every Parent Needs to Know* (Nashville: Thomas Nelson, 2001), 133.

CHAPTER 1 | A RHYTHM OF APPRENTICING
1. Dr. Leonard Sweet, a master wordsmith known for creating new words, was the first person I heard use this concept of being "with-nesses." He asked, "Who are your 'with-nesses'? Who are your friends so that you can be who God called you to be?" For more on this concept, see Leonard Sweet, *11 Indispensable Relationships You Can't Be Without* (Colorado Springs: David C. Cook, 2008).

NOTES

2. I give Tim Elmore credit for revealing Jesus' IDEA for disciplemaking when he discipled me in my early twenties. In 2001, he published his training in *Nurturing the Leader Within Your Child: What Every Parent Needs to Know* (Nashville: Thomas Nelson, 2001), 202.
3. Elizabeth Barrett Browning, *Aurora Leigh*, 1857, bk. 7.
4. Adam Grant, *Think Again: The Power of Knowing What You Don't Know* (New York: Penguin Books, 2023), 80.
5. I've used this inheritance-legacy distinction in equipping disciplemaking relationships and in family ministry for years. Tim Elmore, one of the most influential leaders in my life, was likely the one who introduced me to it. In his book *Nurturing the Leader Within Your Child*, he shares that he first heard it from his friend Reggie Joiner. Elmore, *Nurturing the Leader*, 9.

CHAPTER 2 | A RHYTHM FOR RENEWAL

1. Chris Pierce, vocalist, "Walking on the Earth," by Marvin Etzioni and Richard C. Pierce, track 12 on *Walking on the Earth*, Pierce Records, 2008.
2. My friend Morgan and I have regularly scheduled phone calls with no agenda in which he inevitably offers insight and encouragement. This observation is from one such call.
3. See, for example, John 15:1-4, 16; Romans 7:4; Galatians 5:22-23.
4. Adam Grant, *Think Again: The Power of Knowing What You Don't Know* (New York: Penguin Books, 2023), 4.
5. For example, it's hard not to imagine what Jesus was seeing around Him when He said, "If you have faith as small as a mustard seed, you can say to this mountain, 'Move from here to there,' and it will move. Nothing will be impossible for you" (Matthew 17:20). Or to picture Jesus and the disciples standing on a cliff overlooking Caesarea Philippi when Jesus shared, "I tell you that you are Peter, and on this rock I will build my church, and the gates of Hades will not overcome it" (Matthew 16:18).
6. *Up*, Edward Asner as the voice of Carl, produced by Pixar Animation Studios (Burbank, CA: Walt Disney Studios Home Entertainment, 2009), DVD.

CHAPTER 3 | A RHYTHM OF HOSPITALITY

1. Nick Cave and Seán O'Hagan, *Faith, Hope and Carnage* (New York: Farrar, Straus and Giroux, 2022), 19.
2. Bible Tools, "Strong's #3045: *yada*`," accessed July 16, 2024, https://www.bibletools.org/index.cfm/fuseaction/Lexicon.show/ID/H3045/yada%60.htm.
3. Names have been changed.
4. Name has been changed.

5. Romans 3:23; 5:8; 6:23; 10:9-10, 13.
6. David Lawrence's book *Heaven: It's Not the End of the World* (London: Scripture Union, 1995) was very helpful in shaping my thoughts away from this limited perspective. He outlines a divine purpose for humanity to help restore the world to be closer to what God intended it to be from the beginning.
7. Leonard Sweet, *The Well-Played Life: Why Pleasing God Doesn't Have to Be Such Hard Work* (Orcas Island, WA: Salish Sea Press, 2021), 96.
8. *Paradise*, from Greek *paradeisos*, is used as a name for the Garden of Eden in certain translations of Genesis 2:8. (See, for example, Douay-Rheims 1899 American edition and the Wycliffe Bible.)
9. Alan Hirsch with Darrin Altclass, *The Forgotten Ways Handbook: A Practical Guide for Developing Missional Churches* (Grand Rapids: Brazos Press, 2009), 29.

CHAPTER 4 | A RHYTHM IN COMMUNITY

1. Peter Summerlin, "Magnolia River Ranch," ASLA 2006 Student Awards: Residential Design Award of Honor, American Society of Landscape Architects, accessed July 16, 2024, https://www.asla.org/awards/2006/studentawards/282.html.
2. "May 1, 1969: Fred Rogers Testifies before the Senate Subcommittee on Communications," posted February 8, 2015, by Road Less Marveled, YouTube, 6:50, https://www.youtube.com/watch?v=fKy7ljRr0AA.
3. David Eckman, *Becoming Who God Intended* (Eugene, OR: Harvest House, 2005), 163–64.
4. That the World May Know: Encyclopedia, s.v. "Insulas," accessed September 24, 2024, https://www.thattheworldmayknow.com/category/Encyclopedia?article_page=5&product_page=1.

CHAPTER 5 | A RHYTHM OF COMPASSION

1. According to ClaudeAI, the Hebrew word often rendered "compassion" is *racham*. It appears throughout the Old Testament (Psalm 103:13; Isaiah 49:15; Lamentations 3:22-23). The root *r-ch-m* sometimes refers to the womb and by extension carries the idea of deep, nurturing love akin to the tender feelings a mother has for the child she bears. *Racham* conveys an empathetic, visceral sense of suffering with the one who is going through difficulty or pain.
2. Terry Crist, *Loving Samaritans: Radical Kindness in an Us vs. Them World* (Grand Rapids: Zondervan, 2024), 45.
3. Name has been changed.
4. See, for example, Lindsay Maizland, "Myanmar's Troubled History: Coups, Military Rule, and Ethnic Conflict," Council on Foreign

NOTES

Relations, updated January 31, 2022, https://www.cfr.org/backgrounder/myanmar-history-coup-military-rule-ethnic-conflict-rohingya.

5. My college pastor, Tim Elmore, shared this list with me to explain various manifestations of the Holy Spirit. He also taught this content at Skyline Wesleyan Church in a 1994 sermon series entitled "Who Is This Ghost Called Holy?"
6. See Acts 3:1-10; 7:51-60.
7. See Acts 1:8; 4:1-22, 31; 2 Corinthians 4:13-15.
8. In *Small-Batch Disciplemaking: A Rhythm for Training the Few to Reach the Many* (Colorado Springs: NavPress, 2024), I outline five manifestations of the Holy Spirit, but Tomáš Halík helped me see a sixth manifestation. "The Johannine Pentecost," as some describe this scene in John 20, in which the Spirit is imparted, offers not the "gift of tongues," as in the analogous scene in the Acts of the Apostles, but the language of forgiveness. But this is also above all an instrument for understanding and reaching agreement with people who would otherwise remain strangers to us, or even enemies. Tomáš Halík, *Touch the Wounds: On Suffering, Trust, and Transformation*, trans. Gerald Turner (Notre Dame: University of Notre Dame Press, 2023), 97.
9. *A Beautiful Day in the Neighborhood*, directed by Marielle Heller (2019; Sony Pictures Home Entertainment, 2020). DVD.
10. This concept can also be applied to summertime, especially if you live in an area of mild winters. Many families rely on school-subsidized meals. When school breaks for summer, there's a need for food and snack supplies as well as supplies for summer activities (swim googles, towels, flip-flops, etc.). You can look into summer passes at local public pools, VBS scholarships, and faith-based community partners.

CHAPTER 6 | A RHYTHM OF GENEROSITY

1. Joe Hasell, "From $1.90 to $2.15 a Day: The Updated International Poverty Line," Our World in Data, October 26, 2022, https://ourworldindata.org/from-1-90-to-2-15-a-day-the-updated-international-poverty-line.
2. Proverbs 30:8-9: "Keep falsehood and lies far from me; / give me neither poverty nor riches, / but give me only my daily bread. / Otherwise, I may have too much and disown you / and say, 'Who is the LORD?' / Or I may become poor and steal, / and so dishonor the name of my God." Dr. Lois Tverberg was helpful in introducing me to this possible connection with daily bread. She goes further to suggest that "too many riches may make us forget God, while at the same time, poverty may reduce us to crime." The cost of financial growth then can desensitize a person's heart to not just the needs among them but also the mission of God to bear faithful witness to the world. Lois Tverberg with Bruce Okkema, *Listening to the*

Language of the Bible: Hearing It through Jesus' Ears (Holland, MI: En-Gedi Resource Center, 2004), 98.
3. See Jesus' teaching on the Vine and the branches in John 15:1-17.
4. This idea of trusteeship versus stewardship was something I learned over several conversations with Dr. Leonard Sweet and our doctoral cohort in semiotics, culture, and the church. He's been instrumental in reframing my perspective around gifts, resources, possessions, tithing, and ownership.
5. It's important to understand that incarnation is an ongoing event. Jesus rose so that we can rise. The Incarnation continues in us. "I no longer live, but Christ lives in me" (Galatians 2:20). The Latin phrase *alter Christus, ipse Christus* means "another Christ, Christ Himself." Or, as Saint Augustine put it: "Let us rejoice, then, and give thanks that we are made not only Christians, but Christ. . . . Marvel, be glad, we are made Christ'" (*Homilies on the Gospel of John*, Tractate 21, John 5:20-23, *Nicene and Post-Nicene Fathers*, series 1, ed. Philip Schaff, vol. 7, https://ccel.org/ccel/schaff/npnf107/npnf107.iii.xxii.html). As Leonard Sweet emphasized several times in our doctoral conversations, Jesus wants to live His resurrection life in and through us. The church understands cerebral and intellectual ways more than embodied ways. Truth is a Person who calls us into a relationship. We all have a special agency of living out jubilee in the world. The Good News is not that we can work harder to be more like Jesus; the promise of the Spirit is how we can be born again in unique and different ways. We don't look more similar but distinct.
6. Lara B. Aknin et al., "Happiness Runs in a Circular Motion: Evidence for a Positive Feedback Loop between Prosocial Spending and Happiness," *Journal of Happiness Studies* 13, no. 2 (2012): 347–55, https://www.hbs.edu/faculty/Pages/item.aspx?num=42426, as referenced in Elizabeth W. Dunn et al., "Prosocial Spending and Happiness: Using Money to Benefit Others Pays Off," *Current Directions in Psychological Science* (forthcoming), accessed June 6, 2024, https://dash.harvard.edu/handle/1/11189976.
7. Belle Beth Cooper, "Ten Simple Things You Can Do to Be Happier, Backed by Science," Lifehacker, August 8, 2013, https://lifehacker.com/ten-things-you-can-do-to-be-happier-backed-by-science-1065356587.
8. Martin E. P. Seligman, *Flourish: A Visionary New Understanding of Happiness and Well-Being* (New York: Atria, 2013), 20.
9. I first heard this phrase used by Jim Harbaugh, former coach of the 49ers, to motivate his team. It struck me that this was a great anthem to instill, a perspective of what we do have, not just what we don't. Jim Harbaugh, "Who's Got It Better Than Us?" *The Players' Tribune*, February 1, 2016, https://www.theplayerstribune.com/articles/jim-harbaugh-michigan-football-coach-ann-arbor.

NOTES

CHAPTER 7 | A RHYTHM OF GRATITUDE
1. Robert Robinson, "Come, Thou Fount of Every Blessing," 1758.
2. Hebrew: אֶבֶן הָעֵזֶר. Blue Letter Bible, "Lexicon: Strong's H72—*'eḇen hā'ezer*," accessed September 6, 2024, https://www.blueletterbible.org/lexicon/h72/kjv/wlc/0-1.
3. *Merriam-Webster Dictionary*, s.v. "ebenezer (*n.*)," accessed September 6, 2024, https://www.merriam-webster.com/dictionary/ebenezer.
4. Robinson, "Come, Thou Fount."
5. Robinson, "Come, Thou Fount."
6. Pyloric stenosis is an uncommon condition in infants that blocks food from entering the small intestine.
7. Online Etymology Dictionary, s.v. "enthusiasm (*n.*)," accessed September 24, 2024, https://www.etymonline.com/word/enthusiasm.
8. Luke 19:39-41: "Some of the Pharisees in the crowd said to Jesus, 'Teacher, rebuke your disciples!' 'I tell you,' he replied, 'if they keep quiet, the stones will cry out.' As he approached Jerusalem and saw the city, he wept over it."
9. Strahan Coleman, *Beholding: Deepening Our Experience in God* (Colorado Springs: David C Cook, 2023), 205; Coleman is referencing 1 Corinthians 6:19.
10. My friend and doctoral classmate Kris Clifford was the first one to introduce me to the phrase *arthood of believers* as an alternative perspective to *priesthood of all believers*. Our cohort conversation was around divine imagination and inspired incarnation, trading a service orientation with more generative ways to give of oneself.
11. Like Adam knew Eve or a husband knows his wife. It's not just in the sexual sense but in a "naked and unashamed" sense. I know who Barack Obama is, but I don't know him personally, nor would he recognize me.

CHAPTER 8 | CROWNED AND COMMISSIONED
1. The musical is arranged as a series of parables based on Matthew's Gospel. See *Godspell* the Musical, accessed December 8, 2024, https://www.godspell.com/about-the-show.
2. Adam Grant, *Think Again: The Power of Knowing What You Don't Know* (New York: Penguin Books, 2023), 203.

BOOKS BY DAVID SUNDE

SMALL-BATCH DISCIPLEMAKING
A RHYTHM FOR TRAINING THE FEW TO REACH THE MANY
DAVID SUNDE

HOMEGROWN DISCIPLES
Parenting Rhythms for Drawing Your Kids into Life with God
David Sunde

NavPress
Bold. Loving. Sensible.

AVAILABLE AT NAVPRESS.COM AND WHEREVER BOOKS ARE SOLD